Welcome to
Table Talk

Table Talk helps children and adults explore the Bible together. Each day provides a short family Bible time which, with your own adaptation, could work for ages 4 to 12. It includes optional follow-on material which takes the passage further for older children. There are also suggestions for linking **Table Talk** with **XTB** children's notes.

Who can use Table Talk?

- **Families**
- **One adult with one child**
- **A teenager with a younger brother or sister**
- **Children's leaders with their groups**
- **Any other mix that works for you!**

Table Talk

A short family Bible time for daily use. **Table Talk** takes about five minutes, maybe at breakfast, or after an evening meal. Choose whatever time and place suits you best as a family.

Table Talk includes a simple discussion starter or activity that leads into a short Bible reading. This is followed by a few questions.

XTB

XTB children's notes help 7-11 year olds to get into the Bible for themselves. They are based on the same Bible passages as **Table Talk**. You will find suggestions for how **XTB** can be used alongside **Table Talk** on the next page.

In the next three pages you'll find suggestions for how to use Table Talk, along with hints and tips for adapting it to your own situation. If you've never done anything like this before, check out our web page for further help (see website addresses below) or write in for a fact sheet.

THE SMALL PRINT

Table Talk is published by The Good Book Company, Blenheim House, 1 Blenheim Road, Epsom, Surrey, KT19 9AP, UK Written by Alison Mitchell (alison@thegoodbook.co.uk). Fab pictures by Kirsty McAllister. Bible quotations taken from the Good News Bible. **UK:** www.thegoodbook.co.uk **North America:** www.thegoodbook.com **Australia:** www.thegoodbook.com.au **New Zealand:** www.thegoodbook.co.nz

HOW TO USE
Table Talk

Table Talk is designed to last for up to three month
How you use it depends on what works for you. W
have included 65 full days of material in this issue
plus some more low-key suggestions for another 2
days (at the back of the book). We would like to
encourage you to work at establishing a pattern o
family reading. The first two weeks are the hardes

DAY 1
What shall we do?

> **KEYPOINT**
> When the people heard Peter's
> speech, they asked, "What shall
> we do? **Read Acts 2v38-39**
>
> Today's passages are:
> **Table Talk** Acts 2v38-39
> **XTB** Acts 2v37-40

TABLE TALK Recap: Look again at yesterday's five points from Peter's speech.

READ When the people heard Peter's speech, they asked, "What shall we do?" **Read Acts 2v38-39**

TALK Peter told them to **repent**. What does that mean? (To repent doesn't just mean saying sorry. It means asking God to help you to **change**, and to do what He says.) What two things did Peter say would happen? (Their sins will be forgiven, they'll be given the gift of the Holy Spirit.)

DO Use the illustration in **Notes for Parents** (on the previous page) to show how Jesus rescues us from our sins.

PRAY Verse 39 means that this promise is for **us** too—even though we live 2000 years after Peter! Thank God for sending Jesus so that you can be forgiven.

Building up
The apostles had the task of telling others about Jesus. Some of them also wrote the books that make up the New T. But what if they **forgot** some of what they had seen or heard? Or didn't **understand** it? **Read John 14v25-26** to see how the Holy Spirit helped them. Thank God for making sure that what the apostles taught and wrote down about Jesus was true and accurate.

> **KEYPOINT**
> This is the main point you
> should be trying to convey.
> Don't read this out—it often
> gives away the end of the story!

Table Talk is based on the same Bible passages as *XTB*, but usually only asks for two or three verses to be read out loud. The full *XTB* passage is listed at the top of each **Table Talk** page. If you are using **Table Talk** with older children, read the full *XTB* passage rather than the shorter version.

The main part of **Table Talk** is designed to be suitable for younger children. *Building Up* includes more difficult questions designed for older children, or those with more Bible knowledge.

As far as possible, if your children are old enough to read the Bible verses for themselves, encourage them to find the answers in the passage and to tell you which verse the answer is in. This will help them to get used to handling the Bible for themselves.

The **Building Up** section is optional. It is designed to build on the passage studied in Table Talk (and XTB). Building Up includes some additional questions which reinforce the main teaching point, apply the teaching more directly, or follow up any difficult issues raised by the passage.

Linking with *XTB*

The **XTB** children's notes are based on the same passages as **Table Talk**. There are a number of ways in which you can link the two together:
- Children do **XTB** on their own. Parents then follow these up later (see suggestions below).
- A child and adult work through **XTB** together.
- A family uses **Table Talk** together at breakfast. Older children then use **XTB** on their own later.
- You use **Table Talk** on its own, with no link to **XTB**.

FOLLOWING UP XTB

If your child uses **XTB** on their own it can be helpful to ask them later to show you (or tell you) what they've done. Some useful starter questions are:

- Can you tell me what the reading was about?

- Is there anything you didn't understand or want to ask about?

- Did anything surprise you in the reading? Was there anything that would have surprised the people who first saw it or read about it?

- What did you learn about God, Jesus or the Holy Spirit?

- Is there anything you're going to do as a result of reading this passage?

Table Talk is deliberately not too ambitious. Most families find it quite hard to set up a regular pattern of reading the Bible together—and when they do meet, time is often short. So **Table Talk** is designed to be quick and easy to use, needing little in the way of extra materials, apart from pen and paper now and then.

BUT!!

Most families have special times when they **can** be more ambitious, or do have some extra time available. Here are some suggestions for how you can use **Table Talk** as the basis for a special family adventure...

PICNIC

Take Table Talk with you on a family picnic. Thank God for His beautiful Creation.

WALK

Go for a walk together. Stop somewhere with a good view and read Genesis 1v1—2v4.

GETTING TOGETHER

Invite another family for a meal, and to read the Bible together. The children could make a poster based on the passage.

MUSEUM

Visit a museum to see a display from Bible times. Use it to remind yourselves that the Bible tells us about real people and real history.

HOLIDAYS

Set aside a special time each day while on holiday. Choose some unusual places to read the Bible together—on the beach, up a mountain, in a boat... Take some photos to put on your Table Talk display when you get back from holiday.

You could try one of the special holiday editions of XTB and Table Talk—**Christmas Unpacked, Easter Unscrambled** and **Summer Signposts.**

Have an adventure!

FOOD!

Eat some food linked with the passage you are studying. For example Manna (biscuits made with honey, Exodus 16v31), Unleavened bread or Honeycomb (Matthew 3v4— but don't try the locusts!)

DISPLAY AREA

We find it easier to remember and understand what we learn when we have something to look at. Make a Table Talk display area, for pictures, Bible verses and prayers. Add to it regularly.

VIDEO

A wide range of Bible videos are available—from simple cartoon stories, to whole Gospels filmed with real life actors. (Your local Christian bookshop should have a range.) Choose one that ties in with the passages you are reading together. _**Note:**_ Use the video **in addition** to the Bible passage, not **instead** of it!

PRAYER DIARY

As a special project, make a family prayer diary. Use it to keep a note of things you pray for—and the answers God gives you. This can be a tremendous help to children (and parents!) to learn to trust God in prayer as we see how He answers over time.

Go on—try it!

DRAMA OR PUPPETS

Take time to dramatise a Bible story. Maybe act it out (with costumes if possible) or make some simple puppets to retell the story.

Enough of the introduction, let's get going...

DAYS 1-20
Notes for Parents

DAY 1
Mark it out

MARK'S GOSPEL
Gospel means "good news". Mark's book tells us the good news about Jesus. It's divided into two halves...

🔑 **KEYPOINT**
Jesus' death was part of God's Rescue Plan. God's plans <u>always</u> work out.

Today's passages are:
Table Talk: Mark 14v1-2
XTB: Mark 14v1-2

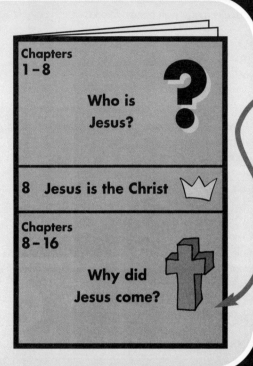

Chapters
1 – 8

Who is Jesus? ?

8 Jesus is the Christ 👑

Chapters
8 – 16

Why did Jesus come?

TABLE TALK — Look at the diagram opposite. We're going to be reading the <u>end</u> of Mark's book. What will it help us to understand? (*Why Jesus came.*)

READ — Jesus had lots of enemies. They wanted to get rid of Him... **Read Mark 14v1-2**

TALK — The chief priests and teachers of the law were religious leaders. But what did they want to do to Jesus? (v1) (*Kill Him.*) It was a special time of year for Jewish people. What festival were they celebrating? (v1) (*Passover*)

Ask your child if they know anything about Passover. (*The first ever Passover meal happened when God rescued Moses and the Israelites from Egypt.*) Passover is all about **Rescue**. That's why Easter happened at Passover time. It's because <u>Easter</u> is all about <u>Rescue</u>, too.

Read about the two plans in **Notes for Parents** opposite.

THE TWO PLANS
The end of Mark's book tells us about the very first Easter. We'll see <u>two</u> very different plans unfolding:
• **The Murder Plot** (Jesus' enemies were plotting to get rid of Jesus by killing Him);
• **God's Rescue Plan** (Amazingly it was always part of God's Rescue Plan that Jesus would die, so that He could <u>rescue</u> His people).

THINK — In the next few weeks we'll be reading about the first Easter. Some of it will be sad, or even horrid. Sometimes it will <u>look</u> like Jesus' enemies are winning. But in the end we'll see that **God** is always in control. His Rescue Plan works out.

PRAY — Thank God that His plans always work out. Ask Him to help you learn about His Rescue Plan as you read Mark.

The Murder Plot

God's Rescue Plan

Building up
Make a poster showing *The Murder Plot* (dark and gloomy) and *God's Rescue Plan* (bright and cheerful). We'll find out more about both plans as we read Mark.

DAY 2
Three reactions

TABLE TALK
Imagine if someone came into the room and poured perfume on your head! How would you each react? (*Discuss.*)

READ
Jesus was having a meal in the home of a man called Simon. While they were eating, a woman came in with a very expensive jar of perfume. She broke the jar, and poured the perfume on Jesus' head. Read how **people reacted**. **Read Mark 14v4-5**

TALK
Were the people pleased? (v4) (*No!*) What did they think should have been done instead? (v5) (*The perfume sold and the money given to the poor.*)

READ
Now see how **Jesus reacted**. **Read Mark 14v6-9**

What did Jesus say she had done? (v6) (*A beautiful thing.*) What did He say the perfume prepared Him for? (v8) (*Burial*)

READ
How did **Judas** (one of Jesus' closest friends) react? **Read Mark 14v10-11**

What did Judas do? (v10) (*Agreed to betray Jesus to the chief priests.*)

What two plans did we learn about yesterday? (*The Murder Plot and God's Rescue Plan.*) It looks like the Murder Plot is winning, but Jesus said the perfume was for His burial. Jesus **knew** He was going to die, and that it was part of God's plan. Thank God that His plans always work out.

PRAY

Building up
Read v9. Jesus said this story would be told all over the world. Have His words come true? (*Yes—the Bible is read all over the world.*) Thank Jesus that His words always come true.

DAY 3
Follow that jar!

TABLE TALK
What important events do you celebrate each year? (*Birthdays, Anniversary, Easter, Christmas, New Year...*) How many of these are celebrated with a meal of some kind?

READ
Jesus wanted to eat a special meal with His disciples. But first they had to get the room ready... **Read Mark 14v12-16**

What meal were they preparing for? (v12) (*Passover*)

DO
(*Optional*) Read more about Passover in **Notes for Parents** on the next page.

TALK
Who were the disciples to follow? (v13) (*A man with a jar of water.*) The two disciples did what Jesus had told them. What did they find? (v16) (*Everything was just as Jesus had told them.*)

Jesus knew this would be His last meal with His disciples. He knew all about the Murder Plot, too! Jesus knew **everything** that would happen.

PRAY
Jesus knows **everything** that happens to you. How does that make you feel? Talk to God about it.

Building up
What evidence is there that Jesus was in control of things? (*He'd clearly made arrangements in advance, so that the man would be there for the disciples to follow, and a room was already set aside for them.*) Jesus knew this would be their last meal together. He made sure they could meet in private.

DAYS 3-5
Notes for Parents

THE PASSOVER

Around 1400 years before Jesus was born, the Israelites were living in Egypt. They were slaves, cruelly treated by Pharaoh the king. So they cried out to God for help.

God sent ten plagues on the Egyptians, and chose <u>Moses</u> to be leader of the Israelites, to rescue them from Egypt and to bring them to the land God had promised them.

Jewish people have celebrated Passover ever since—to remember how God kept His promise and rescued His people.

The Passover Meal

The first ever Passover meal happened on the evening before the Israelites left Egypt. (*See Exodus 12v1-14 for details.*) The meal included roast lamb and unleavened bread (bread without yeast). When Jewish people celebrate Passover today, their meal still includes lamb and unleavened bread. They also dip the bread into bitter herbs (to remember the bitterness of their lives as slaves in Egypt).

WHY DID EASTER HAPPEN AT PASSOVER TIME?

Passover is all about being *rescued*. When Jewish people celebrate the Passover meal they are remembering God's faithfulness in rescuing the Israelites from Egypt.

Ultimately, God's faithfulness in rescuing His people is seen by Him sending His only Son, Jesus, to be our Rescuer. Jesus died on the first Good Friday to save people from their sins.

"You will name Him Jesus—because He will save His people from their sins." *Matthew 1v21*

"Christ Jesus came into the world to save sinners." *1 Timothy 1v15*

DAY 4
Traitor!

KEYPOINT
Nothing and no-one can stop God's perfect plans!

Today's passages are:
Table Talk: Mark 14v17-21
XTB: Mark 14v17-21

TABLE TALK

Play **Hangman** to guess the name 'Judas'. Then ask your child what they know about Judas. (*He was one of Jesus' 12 closest friends; he had agreed to betray Jesus.*)

READ

The rest of the disciples didn't know that Judas was going to betray Jesus. But <u>Jesus</u> did! **Read Mark 14v17-21**

TALK

What surprising news did Jesus tell His friends? (v18) (*One of them would betray Him.*) How did they react? (v19) (*They all said, "Surely not I?"*) But what did Jesus say? (v20) (*It was someone who dipped bread with Jesus—part of the Passover meal; see **Notes for Parents**.*)

The Old Testament writers had said that the 'Son of Man' (a title for Jesus) would die. That's what v21 means. It was <u>always</u> part of God's Rescue Plan.

THINK

Judas did a terrible thing. He would be punished for it later. But Judas couldn't <u>stop</u> God's perfect plans. <u>Nobody</u> can! Instead, Judas himself became part of God's great Rescue Plan!

PRAY

Thank God that **nothing** and **nobody** can stop His perfect plans.

Building up
Find out more about **Judas**:

In **John 13v4-6** we see how Judas reacted to the woman who poured perfume on Jesus' feet, and that Judas was a thief. In **Matthew 27v1-10** we see how Judas' life ended. Notice how this, too, was already in God's plan (v9) and fulfilled words written by Jeremiah hundreds of years earlier.

DAY 5
Ready to be rescued

KEYPOINT
Jesus came to die, to rescue us from our sins. Communion reminds us of this.

Today's passages are:
Table Talk: Mark 14v22-26
XTB: Mark 14v22-26

TABLE TALK

Give yourselves one minute to each find an object that reminds you of something that's happened in the past. (*E.g. photo, holiday souvenir, postcard...*) Talk about the things you found.

READ

We're still reading about Jesus' last meal with His disciples. As you read it, spot two things we use to remember Jesus.
Read Mark 14v22-26

TALK

What did Jesus say the bread was like? (v22) (*His body.*) What was the wine like? (v24) (*His blood.*)

Jesus called the wine 'the blood of the covenant (promise), which is poured out for many'. When do you think Jesus' blood was poured out? (*When He died on the cross.*) What do you think 'poured out for many' means? (*When Jesus died, He died <u>for</u> us [in our place] to take the punishment we deserve. He died to rescue us from our sins. More about this on Day 14.*)

THINK

In churches today, Christians share bread and wine to remember Jesus' death. Why do you think Jesus' followers want to remember His death?

PRAY

Ask God to help you never to forget that Jesus loves you so much that He died to rescue you.

Building up
What could you do to remind you that Jesus died to rescue you? (E.g. make hot cross buns together, draw a poster and copy v24 onto it, make a bookmark for your Bible...)

DAY 6
Standing up for Jesus

KEYPOINT
Jesus said that all His followers would desert Him. Peter denied it, but Jesus was right.

Today's passages are:
Table Talk: Mark 14v27-31
XTB: Mark 14v27-31

TABLE TALK

Have you ever thought you'd be really brave in a situation but when it happened you got really scared? Talk about some times when this has happened.

READ

Jesus told His disciples that they'd all leave Him, like a flock of sheep scattering in panic. But <u>Peter</u> refused to believe it...
Read Mark 14v27-31

TALK

How many times did Jesus say that Peter would deny knowing Jesus? (v30) (*Three times.*) Did Peter believe Jesus? (v31) (*No!*) What did Peter say he would do? (v31) (*Die with Jesus, rather than deny Jesus.*)

Peter <u>thought</u> he knew what would happen. But Jesus <u>really</u> knew what would happen (as we'll see on Day 10).

THINK

Standing up for Jesus can be really hard. We may get laughed at, or even worse. Talk about times when you find it hard to stand up for Jesus.

PRAY

Ask God to help you stand up for Jesus.

Building up
Everything happening to Jesus was written in the Old Testament, long before He was born. This is called <u>prophecy</u>. **Read Zechariah 13v7**. This is quoted in v27 of Mark 14. Who is the shepherd? (*Jesus*) Who are the sheep? (*His followers.*) What would happen? (*They would scatter.*) As we'll see on Day 8, Jesus' friends would scatter, just as the Old T said.

DAY 7
Easy to obey?

KEYPOINT
Jesus knew that a horrible death was waiting for Him. But He chose to obey God.

Today's passages are:
Table Talk: Mark 14v32-36
XTB: Mark 14v32-42

TABLE TALK

What kind of things do you put off if you can? (*E.g. tidying your room, washing up, going to the dentist, saying sorry...*)

READ

In today's reading, Jesus knows that a horrible death is waiting for Him. Let's see if He tried to put it off.
Read Mark 14v32-36

TALK

How was Jesus feeling? (v34) (*Overwhelmed with sorrow.*) What did He ask God His Father to take away? (v36) (*'This cup.'*) Jesus knew that dying on the cross would be like drinking a cup full of suffering. It wasn't easy for Jesus to obey God. But what else did He pray? (v36) (*"Not what I want, but what You want."*)

THINK

It's important to remember that Jesus was always in control. That means He had a <u>choice</u>. He didn't have to die on the cross. He could have chosen not to. Why do you think Jesus chose to obey God and die for us? (*Because He loves us—see 1 John 3v16.*)

PRAY

Give thanks to Jesus for loving us so much that He chose to die for us. Ask God to help you to obey Him too, even when that's hard.

Building up
Read Mark 14v37-42. We've seen that <u>Jesus'</u> choice was to obey God. The <u>disciples</u> had a choice too—to stay awake and pray, or to sleep. Which did they choose? (*To sleep!*) Think of a time when you might find it hard to obey God this week. What might help you to obey God at that time?

DAY 8
Scattering sheep

KEYPOINT
Jesus' followers scattered, just as Jesus (and the Old Testament) had said they would.

Today's passages are:
Table Talk: Mark 14v43-52
XTB: Mark 14v43-52

TABLE TALK

Close your eyes and imagine the scene. It's a Thursday evening—late and dark. Jesus and His disciples are in a quiet garden at the bottom of a hill. Jesus sees lights coming down the hill towards Him. It's a crowd of soldiers, carrying swords and flaming torches. They're coming to get Jesus. What do you think He will do?

READ

Jesus could have escaped, but He didn't. Instead, He waited for the soldiers to arrive—brought by Judas.
Read Mark 14v43-52

TALK

How did Judas betray Jesus? (v44) (*He kissed Jesus.*) How many of Jesus' followers ran away? (v50) (*All of them.*) Does that remind you of anything Jesus had said? (*Jesus told His disciples they'd run away like a flock of sheep scattering in panic—Day 6.*)

THINK

The Murder Plot <u>seemed</u> to be working. But Jesus saw things differently. What did Jesus say was <u>really</u> happening? (v49) (*The Scriptures [Old T] must come true.*) The words in the Old T about Jesus' followers running away like sheep had come true. (*It's in Zechariah 13v7.*) And that's why Jesus didn't escape when He could. He knew that His death was always part of God's Rescue Plan, just as it had been written about in the Old Testament.

PRAY

Thank God that His Rescue Plan worked out exactly as He said it would. Thank Him that His words <u>always</u> come true.

Building up
Read v47 again. Then look up *Luke 22v51* to see what happened to the high priest's servant.

DAY 9
Are you the King?

KEYPOINT
Jesus is the Christ/Messiah
—God's chosen King.

Today's passages are:
Table Talk: Mark 14v60-64
XTB: Mark 14v53-65

TABLE TALK

On 14 small pieces of paper, using three colours of pen, write out the following letters: G,O,D,S (colour 1); C,H,O,S,E,N (colour 2); K,I,N,G (colour 3). Hide the letters round the room. Ask your child to find them, and unjumble them to discover the three words.

READ

Jesus has a special title: **CHRIST** (in Greek) and **MESSIAH** (in Hebrew). Both mean 'God's chosen King'. In today's reading, Jesus is on trial. The High priest wants to know if Jesus is the Christ (Messiah). **Read Mark 14v60-64**

TALK

What did the high priest ask Jesus? (See v61.) What was Jesus' answer? (v62) ("I am.") The high priest refused to believe that Jesus was God's chosen King. He said this was blasphemy (telling lies about God). What did they say should happen to Jesus? (v64) (He should be put to death.)

PRAY

Jesus told the truth about who He is—but the high priest said Jesus was lying. Mark wrote his book so that **we** can know the truth about Jesus. Ask God to help you to learn, understand and believe the truth as you read Mark's book together.

Building up
Read v62 again. What do you think this means? ('Son of Man' is a title for Jesus. The end of Mark tells us that Jesus is now sitting at the right hand of God, His Father [Mark 16v19]. One day, Jesus will come back as our great King, and everyone will see Him!)

DAY 10
Peter peters out

KEYPOINT
Peter denies Jesus, just as Jesus said he would.

Today's passages are:
Table Talk: Mark 14v66-72
XTB: Mark 14v66-72

TABLE TALK

Take it in turns to say "I don't know what you're talking about!" in different accents e.g. Scottish, Australian, Liverpudlian...

READ

In today's story, Peter says this to a servant girl who accuses him of being a friend of Jesus. But Peter's accent gives him away, because he comes from Galilee in the north of Israel (just as Jesus does) and has a northern accent.
Read Mark 14v66-72

DO

(Optional) Read the story again while your child/children act(s) it out.

TALK

How many times did Peter say that he didn't know Jesus? (3) What happened next? (v72) (The cock crowed.) What did this remind Peter of? (v72) (Jesus telling Peter that he would deny Jesus—Day 6) How did Peter react? (v72) (He broke down and wept.)

THINK

Talk about times when you let Jesus down. How do you feel? What should we do when we let Jesus down?

PRAY

Say sorry to Jesus for times when you have let Him down. Ask Him to help you to change and to live for Him.

Building up
Jesus knew that Peter would let Him down. And He was right! Do you think Jesus would trust Peter in the future. Why/why not?

Read John 21v15-17. Jesus forgave Peter. He gave him the job of telling others all about Jesus, and helping them to keep following Jesus. Peter also wrote part of the Bible for us. Do you know which parts? (The New T letters 1&2 Peter.)

DAY 11 Why was Jesus killed?

KEYPOINT
Jesus died to take the punishment for sin that <u>we</u> deserve.

Today's passages are:
Table Talk: Mark 15v6-15
XTB: Mark 15v1-15

TABLE TALK

If your child has played *Cluedo*, ask them what the aim of the game is. (*To find out who the murderer is, what weapon they used, and where e.g. "Miss Scarlet, with the candlestick, in the library."*) Otherwise talk about any mystery story you have read or seen recently.

READ

Jesus is on trial, and about to be sentenced to death. He has been handed over to Pilate, the Roman governor. The question is, "<u>Why</u> was Jesus killed?"
Read Mark 15v6-15

TALK

Every year, Pilate released one prisoner. Who did the crowd want released? (v11) (*Barabbas, a murderer.*) Who stirred them up to ask for Barabbas? (v11) (*The chief priests.*) WHY had the chief priests handed Jesus over to Pilate? (v10) (*Envy.*) What did the crowd want Pilate to do with Jesus? (v13) (*Crucify Him.*) WHY did Pilate agree? (v15) (*To please the crowd.*)

THINK

Jesus <u>didn't</u> die because of envious priests and a governor who wanted to please the crowds! WHY did Jesus die? (*It was God's Rescue Plan.*)

PRAY

Everything that happened was part of God's Rescue Plan. God was always in control. Thank Him for this.

Building up
Barabbas deserved to die and Jesus didn't. But Barabbas was freed whereas Jesus was killed. Jesus took the punishment that Barabbas deserved. **Read Isaiah 53v5-6**, written about Jesus in the Old T, long before He was born. What does it say about us? And about Jesus? So the story about Barabbas reminds us why Jesus died.

DAY 12 King Jesus

KEYPOINT
Jesus is God's chosen King, the Christ/Messiah. We should treat Him as King.

Today's passages are:
Table Talk: Mark 15v16-20
XTB: Mark 15v16-20

TABLE TALK

Imagine that the Queen is coming to visit you in one hour from now. What would you do to get ready?

READ

If we meet a royal person, we tend to treat them in a special way. Jesus had been handed over to some Roman soldiers. They knew that some people believed that Jesus was the King. Read how they treated Jesus.
Read Mark 15v16-20

TALK

What did they give Jesus to wear? (v17) (*A purple robe, and crown of sharp thorns.*) What did they say to Him? (*See v18.*) They also knelt to Jesus—but they were only <u>pretending</u> to believe that Jesus was King. What else did they do? (v19) (*Hit Him on the head and spat on Him.*)

Jesus <u>is</u> God's chosen King. How do **you** want to treat Jesus?

PRAY

Ask God to help you to treat Jesus the right way.

Building up
If Jesus is King of your life, that means that He is in charge. What difference will that make this week at school? at work? with friends? with how you use your time? or money? Pray about these things.

DAY 13
Saving King

KEYPOINT
Jesus <u>didn't</u> save Himself, so that He <u>could</u> save us.

Today's passages are:
Table Talk: Mark 15v24-32
XTB: Mark 15v21-32

TABLE TALK

Recap: What are the two plans we're reading about in Mark? (*The Murder Plot, and God's Rescue Plan.*) As we start to read about Jesus' death, we will read about some horrible things that happened. It might <u>look</u> like the Murder Plot won. BUT remember that **God** was always in control! It was really God's wonderful Rescue Plan that was working out. As we'll see today...

READ

The Roman soldiers nailed Jesus to a cross of wood, and left Him there to die.
Read Mark 15v24-32

TALK

What was written on the notice on Jesus' cross? (v26) (*The King of the Jews.*) As Jesus was dying, many people insulted and mocked Him. What did they shout? (*See v30&v31.*) What did they think Jesus <u>couldn't</u> do? (*Save Himself.*)

THINK

Jesus is the King of everything—so He <u>could</u> have saved Himself! Why didn't He? (*He knew He had come to die, as God's Rescue Plan for His people.*)

PRAY

Jesus <u>didn't</u> save Himself, so that He <u>could</u> save us. Thank King Jesus for dying for you.

Building up

If everything that happened to Jesus was part of God's plan, was it OK for people like Judas, the chief priests, Pilate and the Roman soldiers to make it happen? Why/why not? (*It's hard to understand, but try to help your child see that God can use <u>bad</u> things for His <u>good</u> purposes—and that nothing anyone does can stop God's plans from working out. We won't always understand, but we can **always trust God**.*)

DAY 14
Notes for Parents

MAKE A MODEL (DAY 14)

Make a model of the temple curtain by folding the top of a paper napkin over a short stick or knitting needle. Stick the fold with sticky tape.

At the appropriate point in the story, tear the paper napkin in half, from <u>top</u> to bottom. Spread the two halves apart to show that a way is now open between them.

The Torn Curtain

When Jesus died, the curtain in the temple was torn in two. This <u>wasn't</u> a window curtain! Thus huge curtain separated the rest of the temple from the bit in the middle—where God was said to live. Only the high priest could go in, and only once a year. Nobody else was allowed!

But what happened when Jesus died? (Mark 15v38)

The curtain was t_____ in two.

HOW JESUS RESCUES US

This curtain was a picture of what **sin** does. It reminded people that sin separated them from God. But Jesus came to **rescue** people from the problem of sin!

As Jesus died, all the sins of the world (all the wrongs people do) were put onto Jesus. He took all of our sin onto Himself, taking the punishment we deserve.

When Jesus died, He dealt with the problem of sin. That's why the curtain in the temple was ripped in two, to show that there is <u>nothing</u> to separate us from God any more. Isn't that great news?

DAY 14
God's rescue plan

KEYPOINT
Jesus died so that we no longer have to be separated from God by sin.

Today's passages are:
Table Talk: Mark 15v33-38
XTB: Mark 15v33-38

TABLE TALK

Note: If possible, make a model of the temple curtain as explained in Notes for Parents on the previous page.

READ

When Jesus was on the cross, some very unexpected things happened. They are <u>clues</u> to help us understand why Jesus died. Try to spot them as you read the passage. **Read Mark 15v33-38**

TALK

Jesus was crucified at about 9.00 am. At about noon ("the sixth hour", v33) something odd happened. What? (v33) (_It went totally dark, which lasted for three hours!_) The <u>darkness</u> was a picture of God's <u>anger</u>. He was angry because of **sin**. (_Sin is doing what <u>we</u> want, instead of what <u>God</u> wants. Sin separates us from God._)

Three hours later, Jesus cried out something strange. What was it? (v34) (_"My God, my God, why have you abandoned me?"_) Jesus is God's <u>Son</u>. He has always been close to His Father. But as Jesus died, all the sins of the world were put onto Him. This <u>cut Him off</u> totally from His Father.

What happened just as Jesus died? (v38) (_The temple curtain was torn._) How odd! Turn to **Notes for Parents** on the previous page to find out why.

DO

PRAY

If **you** have been rescued by Jesus, thank Him now. (If you're not sure, who can you talk with to find out more?)

Building up
Take it in turns to explain in your own words why Jesus died. Now think of someone you could explain this to this week.

DAY 15
The watchers

KEYPOINT
Jesus is the Son of God, who died to rescue us. That's why the day He died is called <u>Good</u> Friday.

Today's passages are:
Table Talk: Mark 15v39-41
XTB: Mark 15v39-41

TABLE TALK

(_You need pen and paper._) Write '**Jesus**' in the middle of the paper. How many titles can you think of for Jesus? Write them round His name. (_E.g. Christ, Messiah, LORD, Friend of sinners..._)

READ

Mark's whole book has been about Jesus. Mark has shown us **who** Jesus is and **why** Jesus came. (_If you want, check out the diagram of Mark's book on Day 1._) Now a Roman centurion, who wouldn't have known about the Old T, is going to discover something hugely important about Jesus... **Read Mark 15v39-41**

TALK

What did the centurion say about Jesus? (v39) (_"Surely this man was the Son of God!"_)

DO

Did you have 'Son of God' on your list? If not, add it now.

TALK

Who else was watching as Jesus died? (v40) (_Some women._) These women would see what happened next. We'll meet them again tomorrow.

PRAY

The centurion didn't know much, but he saw Jesus and believed. He was right! Jesus <u>is</u> the Son of God. **Thank God** for sending His Son to rescue you.

Building up
Jesus died on a Friday. What do we call it? (_Good Friday._) Jesus died a horrible, painful death—so why do you think we call it <u>Good</u> Friday? (_Although His death was horrible and sad, Jesus did a <u>good</u> thing when He rescued us from our sin._)

DAY 16
Dead and buried

KEYPOINT
Jesus was definitely dead, and was buried in a stone tomb.

Today's passages are:
Table Talk: Mark 15v42-47
XTB: Mark 15v42-47

TABLE TALK

Yesterday we read about some people who saw Jesus die. Who were they? (*A Roman centurion, and some women.*) Who did the centurion say that Jesus was? (*The Son of God.*)

READ

In today's reading, we'll meet the centurion and the women again...
Read Mark 15v42-47

TALK

Who buried Jesus' body? (v43) (*Joseph, one of Jesus' followers, a rich, powerful man. Note: This isn't Mary's husband.*) Who did Joseph ask for permission to bury Jesus? (v43) (*Pilate, the Roman governor.*) Who did Pilate check with first? (v44) (*The centurion.*) Who was watching? (v47) (*Two Marys.*)

THINK

These people all knew for sure that Jesus was dead. But they had no idea what would happen next! Do you?

Actually, Jesus <u>had</u> told His friends beforehand what would happen to Him, but they didn't understand. (*Optional—read Jesus' words in Mark 14v28.*)

PRAY

Like Jesus' friends, we sometimes find it hard to understand what God is telling us in the Bible, or to believe that He'll do what He says. Ask God to help you to understand and believe His promises.

Building up
Sometimes, non-believers try to explain the resurrection appearances (people seeing Jesus <u>after</u> the crucifixion) by claiming that Jesus never actually died. What evidence is there in this passage that Jesus was definitely dead?

DAY 17
He's not here...

KEYPOINT
Jesus had said He would come back to life—and He did! Jesus is still alive today.

Today's passages are:
Table Talk: Mark 16v1-8
XTB: Mark 16v1-8

TABLE TALK

What day of the week did Jesus die on? (*Friday*) The Saturday was the <u>Sabbath</u>, a Jewish day of rest. Nobody was allowed to go near a dead body on the Sabbath. So Jesus' friends couldn't go near the tomb until early on Sunday morning.

THINK

Three women took spices to put on the body. Why did they know where to go? (*They'd seen Him buried there—Mark 15v47.*) What did they expect to find? (*Jesus' body.*)

READ

They didn't find what they expected! **Read Mark 16v1-8**

TALK

Who did the women see? (v5) (*A young man in white—he was an angel.*) What did he tell the women? (v6) (*"He is not here. He has risen!"*) But the women were terrified. What did they do? (v8) (*Ran away, and told no-one.*)

(<u>Optional</u>—compare v7 with Mk 14v28.)

Jesus had <u>said</u> that He would come back to life—and He did!

PRAY

The New T also says Christians will rise again, with perfect bodies, to live with Jesus forever. Hard to believe? Then pray yesterday's prayer again.

Building up
Read v7 again. Which disciple was mentioned by name? (*Peter*). Why do you think it was important that Peter knew he was included, and that Jesus wanted to see him, too? (*Maybe because Peter had denied Jesus, and now thought that Jesus wouldn't want him any more.*) What a lovely example of God's kindness to His people!

DAYS 18-20
Notes for Parents

THE END OF MARK

Mark wrote his book to show us **who** Jesus is and **why** Jesus came.

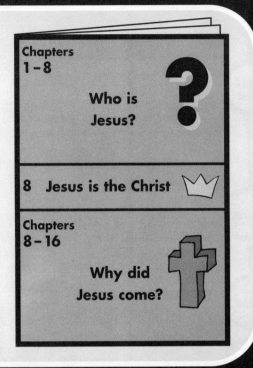

Chapters
1–8

Who is Jesus?

8   Jesus is the Christ

Chapters
8–16

Why did Jesus come?

Have a look at your Bible to see what's printed just after verse 8 of chapter 16.

Your Bible probably has a line or some extra words between v8 and v9. That's because some people think that **Mark** finished writing his book at v8 (with the women running away from the empty tomb), and that **someone else** added v9-20 later.

Verses 9-20 tell us what happened next. They tell us things we can also read in other parts of the Bible. For example, v9-14 tell us about Mary Magdalene and others seeing Jesus after His resurrection. You can also read about this in **Matthew 28v1-10** and **Luke 24v13-39**.

Verses 9-20 of chapter 16 may not have been written by Mark himself—but they are a good summary of what happened next.

DAY 18
What happened next

KEYPOINT
Jesus rose again from the dead, and is still alive today.

Today's passages are:
Table Talk: Mark 16v9-14
XTB: Mark 16v9-14

TABLE TALK
Recap yesterday's story: Who went to the tomb? (*Three women.*) Was Jesus' body there? (*No*) Who was there? (*An angel.*) What did the angel tell them? (*Jesus had risen from the dead.*)

READ
Yesterday's reading ended with the incredible news that Jesus was alive! But nobody had seen Him yet...
Read Mark 16v9-14

TALK
Who saw Jesus first? (v9) (*Mary Magdalene.*) Did the others believe her? (v11) (*No*) Who saw Jesus next? (v12) (*Two people.*) Did the others believe them? (v13) (*No*) Who saw Jesus next? (v14) (*The eleven disciples.*) What did Jesus do? (v14) (*He told them off, because they had refused to believe that He was alive.*)

THINK
Do you think it was easy to believe Jesus had come back to life? Why/why not?

John's Gospel tells us that **Thomas** (one of the disciples) refused to believe it until he had seen and touched Jesus for himself. Check out what Jesus said to Thomas in **John 20v29**.

PRAY
Jesus was talking about you and me! If **you** believe that Jesus came back to life and is still alive today, then **thank God** for <u>giving</u> you that belief.

Note: If you find it hard to believe, there's loads of other evidence in the Bible. Think of someone (maybe an older Christian from your church?) who could help you to think about this.

Building up
Read **Notes for Parents** to find out more about these last verses in Mark.

DAY 19
Chatterboxes

KEYPOINT
Jesus wants us to be chatterboxes about Him.

Today's passages are:
Table Talk: Mark 16v15-16
XTB: Mark 16v15-18

TABLE TALK

Take it in turns to be a chatterbox for 30 seconds. You have to talk non-stop about a subject (e.g. spiders, chocolate, things that make you laugh, mobile phones, turnips...)

READ

Jesus wanted His followers to be chatterboxes! **Read Mark 16v15-16**

TALK

<u>What</u> did Jesus want His followers to tell people? (v15) (*The gospel/good news.*) <u>Who</u> was that good news about? Check back to **Mark 1v1** to see. (*It's the good news about Jesus.*) <u>Where</u> was the good news about Jesus to be taught? (v15) (*The whole world.*)

THINK

What does Jesus say will happen to those who believe? (v16) (*They will be saved.*) What will happen to those who don't believe? (*They will be condemned /punished.*) The **only** way for someone to be rescued from sin and be friends with God is by <u>believing in Jesus</u>. You can see why it's so important to be chatterboxes about Jesus!

PRAY

Jesus wants you and me to be chatterboxes about Him too. And that means that He will <u>help</u> us to do it. Pray together about that now.

Building up
Read Mark 16v17-18. Jesus' disciples <u>did</u> become chatterboxes about Him. And the kinds of things listed in v17-18 did happen, as signs that everything the disciples taught about Jesus was true. Can you think of any examples from the book of Acts? (*E.g. Acts 2v4, 3v7, 28v5.*)

DAY 20
Up, up and away

KEYPOINT
Jesus is still alive, and one day will come back. Meanwhile, we're to tell people about Him.

Today's passages are:
Table Talk: Mark 16v19-20
XTB: Mark 16v19-20

TABLE TALK

I used to teach the Bible in schools. One day, a boy asked me "When did Jesus die again?" He was asking when Jesus died for the *second* time. What would you say to him? (*Jesus <u>didn't</u> die a second time. He's still alive today.*)

READ

Jesus didn't die a second time—but He didn't stay on earth either! **Read Mark 16v19-20**

Where did Jesus go? (v19) (*To heaven.*)

DO

(*Optional*) Read more about this in **Acts 1v9-11**.

THINK

One day, Jesus will <u>come back</u> again. (This is in Acts 1v11.) What do you think we should do while we're waiting? Talk about your ideas. (*Live the way Jesus wants us to, and tell others about Him.*)

DO

Each think of someone you would like to tell about Jesus. (*It might be good to write their names on a list, and put it somewhere you'll see it as you do Table Talk.*) Think of some ways you could tell them about Jesus. (*E.g. tell them something you learnt while using Table Talk, or invite them to come to your church or Christian group with you, or tell them you'd like to pray for them, or...*)

PRAY

Now ask God to help you to do this.

Building up
If you'd like help telling your friends about Jesus, please **write** to The Good Book Company at the address on page 1 or **email** me at: alison@thegoodbook.co.uk

DAYS 21-35
Notes for Parents

DAY 21
The Real King

THE BOOK OF 1 SAMUEL

1 Samuel and **2 Samuel** are really just <u>one</u> book. But it was such a BIG book, that it was split into two parts.

1 Samuel follows straight on from the book of **Judges**. In it we meet the very <u>last</u> Judge. Can you guess his name? (*Samuel!*)

HANNAH'S STORY
(Day 22)

Elkanah had two wives ~ Hannah and Peninnah.

Peninnah had <u>lots</u> of children. But Hannah had <u>none</u>.

Each year, the family went to God's temple at Shiloh. They worshipped God there.

But, every year, Peninnah teased Hannah because she had no children.

This upset Hannah so much that she'd cry and not eat

One year, Hannah was terribly upset. She went to the temple to pray.

KEYPOINT
1 Samuel follows straight on from Judges. 1 Samuel shows that **God** is the Real King.

Today's passages are:
Table Talk: Judges 21v25
XTB: Judges 21v25

TABLE TALK

Find out about the book of *1 Samuel* in **Notes for Parents**.

READ

1 Samuel follows on from the book of *Judges*. So let's set the scene by looking at the last verse of Judges.
Read Judges 21v25

TALK

This verse is about God's special people, the Israelites. What does it say the people were doing? (*The people did as they saw fit/as they pleased.*) The Israelites weren't <u>obeying</u> anyone—they just did what they felt like. But they were God's people, so who <u>should</u> they have obeyed? (*God*)

THINK

What does v25 say the Israelites don't have? (*A king.*) For the last 400 hundred years the Israelites had been led by people called Judges. So it's true that they didn't have a <u>man</u> as king. But they **did** have a King. Who do you think the **real King** of the Israelites was? (*God*)

PRAY

In 1 Samuel we will see that **God** is the Real King, and that He is the One to obey. Ask God—the Real King—to help you learn more about Him as you read 1 Samuel.

Building up

Do you know the names of any of the Judges? Flick through the book of Judges to spot the stories of Ehud, Deborah, Gideon and Samson. God was **hugely kind** to the Israelites. He sent Judges to rescue them from their enemies, even though they didn't deserve it. But sadly the people kept **turning away** from God, again and again and again. We'll see whether they do the same in 1 Samuel...

DAY 22
Pray Day

KEYPOINT
Hannah prayed for a son. Eli told her that God would give her what she asked.

Today's passages are:
Table Talk: 1 Samuel 1v12-18
XTB: 1 Samuel 1v1-18

TABLE TALK

Think of some different ways to pray. (E.g. aloud, quietly in your head, sung prayers, memorised prayers such as the Lord's prayer, written in a prayer diary...)

Today's story is about an unhappy woman who prays for help. Read about her in the cartoon in **Notes for Parents** opposite.

READ

When Hannah was in the temple, she prayed to God, and asked Him to give her a son. Hannah prayed quietly in her head, but moved her lips as she prayed. Eli the priest was watching Hannah. He saw her moving her lips, but not speaking aloud. Eli didn't think she was praying...

Read 1 Samuel 1v12-18

TALK

What did Eli think when he saw Hannah? (v13) (*That she was drunk!*) But Hannah wasn't drunk! When she told Eli about her prayer, what did he say? (v17) (*"May God give you what you've asked Him for."*) What difference did this make to Hannah? (v18) (*She was no longer sad.*)

PRAY

We can talk to God about anything, just as Hannah did. And you can pray in any of the ways you listed earlier. God won't always answer in the way we **expect**—but He'll always answer in the way that's **best.** Ask God to help you to pray about everything, and to trust His answers.

Building up
Eli was God's priest, and spoke for God. He told Hannah that God would give her what she had asked for. But God doesn't always give us what we ask! Why not? (*He always gives us what's **best** for us—and unlike us, God always knows what's best.*)

DAY 23
Given back to God

KEYPOINT
God answered Hannah's prayer. Everything is possible for God.

Today's passages are:
Table Talk: 1 Samuel 1v11&19-20
XTB: 1 Samuel 1v19-20

DO

Use a tape measure to measure how long each person's hair is. Whose is longest?

READ

Yesterday we learnt that Hannah asked God for a son. Read part of Hannah's prayer in **1 Samuel 1v11**.

TALK

What did Hannah say she would not do? (*Not cut her son's hair.*) Does that sound odd? Can you think of anyone else in the Bible who never cut his hair? (*Samson*)

In Bible times, not cutting your hair showed that you would serve God in a special way. Hannah told God that if He gave her a son, she would *give her son back to God*, to serve God all his life. His long hair would be a sign of this.

READ

Let's see how God answers Hannah's prayer. **Read 1 Samuel 1v19-20**

What did Hannah call her son? (v20) (*Samuel*) Why? (v20) (*Because she asked God for him—Samuel means "heard or asked of God".*)

PRAY

Wow! Hannah had never been able to have children. But now she had a son! **God** had made it possible. Thank God that everyone is possible for Him.

Building up

Not cutting your hair was a sign of serving God as a **Nazirite**. Read more about this in **Judges 13v5** and **Numbers 6v1-8**.

DAY 24
A promise kept

KEYPOINT
Hannah kept her promise to give her son back to God. She knew that <u>God</u> must come first.

Today's passages are:
Table Talk: 1 Samuel 1v26-28
XTB: 1 Samuel 1v21-28

Recap: Do you remember Hannah's prayer? Think of <u>two</u> things Hannah promised God. (*Not to cut her son's hair, and to give her son back to God.*)

Hannah promised to give her son <u>back to God</u>. She would do this by taking Samuel to live in the temple with Eli the priest. Samuel would grow up, live and work in the temple—serving God. But Hannah couldn't do this while Samuel was a tiny baby. Why not? (*He would need looking after, and was still drinking his mother's milk.*) Hannah waited until Samuel was **weaned** (stopped drinking breast milk) before taking him to live in the temple. In Bible times, children were weaned when they were about <u>three</u> years old.

Hannah took young Samuel to Eli in the temple. **Read 1 Samuel 1v26-28**

What did Hannah remind Eli about? (v26) (*The time he saw her praying.*) Did Hannah keep her promise to give Samuel back to God? (v28) (*Yes*) How do you think she <u>felt</u> as she left Samuel?

It must have been hard for Hannah to leave the son she'd wanted for ages. But she'd <u>promised</u> to give Samuel to God, and she knew **God must come first!**

Ask God to help <u>you</u> to put Him first too, even when that's hard.

Building up
Do you know anyone with a small baby? Pray that their child will grow up to know and love God. And pray that they will always put God first (as Hannah did), even when that's hard.

DAY 25
Hannah's story

KEYPOINT
Hannah thanked God for what He had <u>done</u> for her and what He is <u>like</u>. So should we.

Today's passages are:
Table Talk: 1 Samuel 2v1-3
XTB: 1 Samuel 2v1-10

<u>Note:</u> Hannah's prayer in v1-10 is quite hard to understand, so copy this simpler version onto some paper. Today's questions can be based on this version:

"The LORD has filled my heart with joy. No-one is holy (perfect) like the LORD. No-one is a Rock like our God. The LORD knows everything." (v1-3)

Read 1 Samuel 2v1-3 and see how each verse matches with the words you wrote down.

Look at each sentence in the prayer you wrote down. Talk about <u>why</u> you think Hannah would have prayed it. E.g. How had God filled Hannah's heart with joy? (*By giving her a son.*)

The rest of Hannah's prayer praises God for what He is **like**. He gives <u>strength</u> to the weak, and <u>food</u> to the hungry (v4-5); He is in <u>control</u> of the whole world (v8); He <u>protects</u> His people (v9).

Hannah knows that God has answered her prayer and given her Samuel, and that God is in control of the whole world. She knows that God is the **Real King**.

Hannah not only thanked God for what He'd <u>done</u>, but for what He is <u>like</u>. She could <u>trust</u> Him because she <u>knew</u> Him well. How can **you** get to know what God is like? Ask Him to help you.

Building up
Read the whole of Hannah's prayer in **v1-10**. Each choose one verse that particularly strikes you, and tell the others why you chose it. Then turn these things into prayer.

DAY 26
One, two, three

KEYPOINT
Samuel served God, but Eli's sons were wicked. God kindly gave Hannah five more children.

Today's passages are:
Table Talk: 1 Samuel 2v12&18-21
XTB: 1 Samuel 2v11-21

TABLE TALK

ONE SON: Ask your child what they remember about **Samuel**. (*He was born after Hannah prayed for a son. Hannah gave him back to God, to serve God in the temple with Eli the priest.*)

READ

TWO SONS: Eli the priest had <u>two</u> sons. Read about them in **1 Samuel 2v12**

What were Eli's sons like? (*Wicked men who didn't care about God.*)

THREE SONS (and two daughters!):
Read 1 Samuel 2v18-21

TALK

How was <u>Samuel</u> different from <u>Eli's sons</u>? (v18) (*Samuel was serving God ['ministering'], but Eli's sons didn't care about God.*) Samuel wore an **ephod** (a sleeveless tunic). What did Hannah make for Samuel each year? (v19) (*A little robe.*) Eli the priest told Hannah that God would give her more children. How many did God give her? (v21) (*Three sons and two daughters.*)

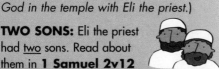

PRAY

Hannah gave up her one son to serve God. But she wasn't left alone. God gave her five more children! Doing what is right may mean giving up something—but trust God. He is so kind!

Building up
Read 1 Samuel 2v12-17. God had given instructions about how sacrifices (gifts) should be offered to God. Part of the meat was to be food for the priests— but only <u>after</u> it had been offered to God. Eli's sons helped themselves to the best of the meat, <u>before</u> giving any to God! More about Eli's wicked sons tomorrow...

DAY 27
Samuel sandwich

KEYPOINT
Samuel was very different from Eli's sons. Which of them are <u>you</u> like?

Today's passages are:
Table Talk: 1 Samuel 2v22-26
XTB: 1 Samuel 2v22-26

TABLE TALK

If possible, make a triple sandwich to help your child understand today's verses.

This part of 1 Samuel is like a triple decker **Samuel Sandwich!** It's been written like that to point out the HUGE difference between Samuel and Eli's sons.

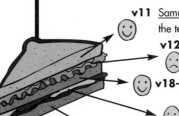

v11 <u>Samuel</u> is serving God in the temple

v12-17 <u>Eli's two sons</u> are breaking God's laws

v18-21 <u>Samuel</u> is serving God

v22-25 Everyone knows about <u>Eli's sons</u>

v26 <u>Samuel</u> is growing up to love and serve God

READ

First, let's look at the <u>sandwich filling</u>. It's all about Eli's sons. Yesterday we saw that they were **wicked** men (v12). But there's more... **Read 1 Samuel 2v22-26**

TALK

Did Eli know his sons were breaking God's laws? (v22) (*Yes*) Who else knew? (v23-24) (*Everyone*) Eli warned his sons that no-one could help them if they kept on breaking God's laws. Did Eli's sons listen to him? (v25) (*No*)

But what about Samuel? (He's the <u>bread</u> in the sandwich!) What's **he** like? (v11,18,26) (*Growing up to love and serve God.*)

PRAY

Pray
Which of these people are <u>you</u> like?

Are you ever like **Eli's sons**? You know you <u>should</u> please God, but instead you <u>keep</u> disobeying Him? If so, be honest with God. Tell Him you're sorry and ask Him to help you change.

Are you like **Samuel**? Do you try to please God and live for Him? If so, <u>thank God</u> for helping you be like this. Ask Him to help you grow up to be someone who serves God with your whole life.

DAY 28
Sin matters

KEYPOINT
Sin matters. The right
punishment for sin is death.

Today's passages are:
Table Talk: 1 Samuel 2v27-29
XTB: 1 Samuel 2v27-36

TABLE TALK

Recap: What were Eli's sons like?
(*Wicked—they didn't care about God.*)

Eli and his sons were priests from the family line of Aaron. As priests, they were allowed to eat some of the meat offered to God as sacrifices (gifts). But Eli's sons had been helping themselves to the **best** of the meat! Eli told his sons off, but he <u>didn't</u> stop them being priests. So God sent a messenger (prophet) to tell Eli what would happen.
Read 1 Samuel 2v27-29

TALK

Who did Eli honour the most—God or his sons? (v29) (*His sons.*) Eli had put his <u>sons</u> before <u>God</u>, when he let them disobey God. The rest of God's message told Eli what would happen next (v30-36):
• Eli's family would <u>no longer</u> be priests;
• Eli's sons would both <u>die</u> on the same day;
• God would provide a <u>new priest</u> who would love and serve God.

THINK

Sin matters! The right punishment for sin is <u>death</u>. But the great news of the Bible is that God has sent us a **Rescuer**, to solve the problem of sin. Find out more in **Notes for Parents** opposite.

PRAY

Thank God for sending Jesus to rescue everyone who believes in Him.

Building up
Read 1 Samuel 2v25. The right punishment for sin is <u>death</u>. But that's not the shocking part of this verse. <u>Why</u> wouldn't Eli's sons listen to their father's warning? (*Because God had decided to put them to death.*) It is possible to be so determined to keep sinning, that God will make us stick to that choice, and punish us accordingly. (*There is similar teaching in Romans 1v18-32, where God "gave them up" to the way of life they so eagerly desired—v24,26,28.*) Pray with your child that they (and you) will have a right understanding of the seriousness of sin, and a genuine desire to love and serve God, rather than rebel against Him.

THE BOOK ILLUSTRATION

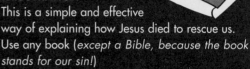

This is a simple and effective way of explaining how Jesus died to rescue us. Use any book (*except a Bible, because the book stands for our sin!*)

Hold up your <u>right hand</u>. Explain that your hand represents you, and that the ceiling stands for God. Show the book, and ask them to imagine that it contains a record of your **sin**—every time you have done, said or thought things that are wrong. Put the book flat on your right hand.

Ask: "What does the book do?"
It <u>separates</u> you from God. This is a picture of what **sin** does. It gets in the way between us and God, and stops us knowing Him as our Friend. The final result of sin is <u>death</u>. You can see why we need rescuing!

Now hold up your <u>left hand</u>. This stands for Jesus. Jesus lived a perfect life. He never sinned. There was <u>nothing</u> separating Jesus from God.

Explain that as Jesus died on the cross, the sin of the whole world was put onto Him. *Transfer the book from your right hand to your left hand to show this.*

Ask: "What is there between Jesus and God?"
The answer is—Your sin!
This is why Jesus died—to take the punishment for all our sin. He died in our place.

Now look back at your right hand.
Ask: "What is there between me and God?"
The answer is—Nothing!

When Jesus died on the cross, He took the punishment for our sins so that we can be forgiven. This means that there is <u>nothing</u> to separate us from God any more. This was **God's Rescue Plan** for us.

DAY 29
Wake up call

Today's passages are:
Table Talk: 1 Samuel 3v1-10&15-18
XTB: 1 Samuel 3v1-18

TABLE TALK

What can you hear from your bed?

One night, when young Samuel was in bed, he heard someone calling him...
Read 1 Samuel 3v1-10

DO

(Optional) Act out the story together.

TALK

Who did Samuel think was calling him? (v5) (Eli) Who was really calling Samuel? (v10) (God) After the third time, Eli realised that it was **God** calling Samuel. What did Eli tell Samuel to say?

Samuel!

(v9) ("Speak, Lord, your servant is listening.")

READ

God did speak. But His words were hard. God told Samuel that the time was soon coming when God would punish Eli's family for disobeying Him. (v11-14) Not surprisingly, Samuel didn't want to tell Eli... **Read 1 Samuel 3v15-18**

TALK

What did Eli say? (v18) ("He is the Lord; let Him do what is good in His eyes.") Eli totally accepted God's word, even though it was really tough on him.

PRAY

God's ways are always **best**. God's words are always **good** and **right**, and always come **true**. Thank God that He's like this. Ask Him to help you accept that His ways are always right and good.

Building up
Read God's message in **v11-14**. God had already sent a prophet to tell Eli about the punishment that was coming (2v27-36). Why do you think God now uses Samuel as His messenger? (There's a clue in 3v1, v7 & v21.) (Samuel is going to bring God's Word to the people. This is the start of that ministry.) More about this tomorrow...

DAY 30 Return of the Word

Today's passages are:
Table Talk: 1 Samuel 3v1&19-21
XTB: 1 Samuel 3v19-21

TABLE TALK

Take it in turns to mime different ways of sending messages. E.g. writing a letter, telephoning, email, semaphore... The others try to guess what you're miming.

READ

Read 1 Samuel 3v1

In those days, how often did God speak to the Israelites? (v1) (Rarely)

The Israelites had stopped listening to God, so He didn't speak to them much any more. But God is **so good** to His people that He's going to start speaking to them again— through **Samuel**.

READ

Read 1 Samuel 3v19-21

What did all the people know about Samuel? (v20) (He was a prophet [God's messenger], telling people God's word to them.) Who did God's word come to? (3v21 & 4v1) (To all Israel, through Samuel.)

PRAY

Today, God still speaks to us through His Word. The **Bible** is God's Word to us. We can learn more about God, and get to know Him better, by reading the Bible. **Thank God** for the Bible. **Ask Him** to help you to understand what you read, and get to know Him better through it.

Building up
Read 2 Timothy 3v16-17. Find six things these verses tell you about the Bible.

DAY 31
Ark ahoy

KEYPOINT
God allows the Israelites to be defeated. He has something important to teach them.

Today's passages are:
Table Talk: 1 Samuel 4v1-4
XTB: 1 Samuel 4v1-4

Draw a picture or make a model of the Ark of the Covenant. You can find out about the ark in **Building Up** below.

The Israelites are fighting their enemies the Philistines. No problem—God always gives them victory. Doesn't He???
Read 1 Samuel 4v1-4

Did the Israelites win? (v2) (*No!*) What question did they ask? (v3) (*"Why did the LORD bring defeat on us today?"*) What did they decide to bring to the battle field? (v4) (*The ark.*) Who came with the ark? (v4) (*Eli's two sons.*) What do you remember about Eli's sons? (*They were wicked men, who didn't care about God. God had said that their punishment would be death.*)

Who is the **Real King**? (*God*) **God** is in charge of what's happening. He is going to teach the Israelites something very important. Ask God to help you to learn important things about Him, too, as you read 1 Samuel.

Building up
The Ark of the Covenant (the Covenant Box) was a wooden box, covered in gold. Inside the ark were two stone tablets with the Ten Commandments written on them. The ark reminded the Israelites that **God was with them**.

DAY 32
Lucky ark?

KEYPOINT
The ark was captured and Eli's two sons were killed—just as God had said they would be.

Today's passages are:
Table Talk: 1 Samuel 4v5-7&10-11
XTB: 1 Samuel 4v5-11

What things do people have or do to get lucky? (*E.g. lucky toy, special necklace, touch wood...*)

Read 1 Samuel 4v5-7

What did the Israelites do when the ark arrived? (v5) (*Gave a great shout.*) How did the Philistines feel? (v7) (*Afraid*)

The Philistines thought that 'a god' had come, so they decided to fight extra hard... **Read 1 Samuel 4v10-11**

Who won the battle? (v10) (*Philistines*) What happened to the ark? (v11) (*It was captured.*) What happened to Eli's two sons? (v11) (*They died.*)

Earlier, the Israelites had asked "Why did the Lord bring defeat on us today?" (v3). How would you answer their question?

It's a good question, but the Israelites hadn't waited for the answer! Instead, they used the ark like a lucky charm. They thought God would have to give them victory, because the ark was there. But God doesn't work that way. We can't tell Him what to do!!! He's the King!

We should trust God because He's in control even when things go wrong for us. God used this defeat to teach His people something important. Ask God to help you learn when bad things happen.

Building up
Read v11 again. Why did Eli's sons die? (*Because God had said they would.*) Look back to **1 Samuel 2v25** and **2v34**. God's words always come true. How does that make you feel? Talk to Him about it.

DAY 33
No glory

KEYPOINT
Eli and his daughter-in-law both died believing that God had left Israel.

Today's passages are:
Table Talk: 1 Samuel 4v19-22
XTB: 1 Samuel 4v12-22

TABLE TALK

The Israelites had been defeated, and the ark captured. Now the news had to be taken to Shiloh, where Eli the priest was waiting. Read the cartoon story in **Notes for Parents** opposite.

READ

Eli's death wasn't the last one on that sad day... **Read 1 Samuel 4v19-22**

TALK

Eli's daughter-in-law died giving birth to her son. What did she call him? (v21) (*Ichabod*) Ichabod means 'no glory'. What did his mother say? (v22) (*"The glory has left Israel because the ark of God has been captured."*)

THINK

What did the ark remind the Israelites of? (*It's in **Building Up** on Day 31.*) The ark reminded the Israelites that *God was with them*. But now the ark had been captured! So both Eli and his daughter-in-law died thinking that God had left Israel. *But this isn't the end of the story, as we'll see tomorrow...*

PRAY

Don't worry! If you're a Christian, God has promised that He will never leave you. **Thank God** that He never leaves His people. (*This promise is in Building Up below, if you want to look it up.*)

Building up
Look up God's promise in **Deuteronomy 31v6**. What will God never do? (*Leave or abandon His people.*) This promise was made to Joshua thousands of years ago. But the writer of Hebrews says that it applies to us as well. **Read Hebrews 13v5**. This is true for all Christians.

After the Battle

An Israelite soldier ran from the battle field all the way to Shiloh.

He told the whole town what had happened.

Eli was waiting for news. He was worried about the ark.
What's all this noise about?
What has happened?

The man told Eli his news.
The Philistines beat us!
Your sons Hophni and Phinehas are both dead.

And the ark has been captured!

When Eli heard about the ark, he fell off his chair.
His neck was broken, and he died.

This story is in 1 Samuel 4v12-18.

Sing Hosanna!

Most parents naturally sing songs with little children—lullabies to get them to sleep, silly songs to make them laugh, and action songs to get them moving around.

Often, however, as they get older, we do it less and less. Perhaps we are embarrassed by our own 'less than perfect' abilities, or it could be that we view it as childish. Whatever the reason, I want to encourage you to continue singing with your kids as they grow older (or to restart it) for a number of very good reasons.

WHY BOTHER WITH SINGING?

★ **BECAUSE IT'S COMMANDED:** Ephesians 5v19 says: 'Speak to one another with psalms, hymns and spiritual songs. Sing and make music in your heart to the Lord...' Singing, it seems, is not an optional extra in the Christian life; all Christians in every age have done it. Some of the world's greatest music has come from the desire to praise and glorify God in song. Singing is a vital part of the way Christians operate together. And that's for a good reason...

★ **BECAUSE IT HELPS US REMEMBER THE BIBLE:** Something about the marriage of lyrics and a tune makes words so much more memorable. You probably have stashed away in your head thousands of song lyrics that will be called to mind as soon as you hear a snatch of the melody. Song is a fantastic way of remembering Bible truth and of memorising great chunks of the Bible.

★ **BECAUSE IT NURTURES FAITH:** Singing truths about God helps us to express our faith and trust in Christ to each other. Children, most of the time, sit and receive information about God. But as the old saying goes: 'Expression deepens Impression'. As we express the truths of the Gospel we start to really understand and believe them. Music has the ability to stir our emotions, and make the vital connection between our head and our heart.

★ **BECAUSE IT'S ENCOURAGING:** Paul and Silas in prison, having received a thorough beating, did what? They sang hymns to God. (Acts 16 v 25) And not just to keep their spirits up; the verse also says that the other prisoners were listening to them—it was evangelistic!

Singing is wonderfully encouraging, not only from the warm feeling of hearing others, but from the **content** of the songs. When we sing, we remind ourselves and each other of the great truths of the Gospel: of God's love for us; of God's great purposes in the world; of the glory of heaven. By teaching and singing songs with your children, you will store up within them an easily remembered treasure house of Bible knowledge.

★ **BECAUSE IT'S FUN:** If we are embarrassed by singing, then we will pass that on to our children. Most of us (even if we have a *terrible* voice) love to sing in the bath or shower when no-one is around. We do it because it's fun! Maybe we can conquer some of our inhibitions a little, if we understand how valuable it can be to make learning Bible truth enjoyable for our children.

WHAT TO SING

Because music is so powerful emotionally it makes a good ally for us as we try to nurture the faith of our young ones. But that same strength is also its great weakness. Music can be used to manipulate, and teach error. So here are a couple of pointers:

★ **SING TRUTH!** Make sure that the songs you regularly sing have accurate Bible truth, and teach the right things. We have listened to some children's songs CDs with awful content. The problem is, it tends to be mixed in with good stuff, so it can sneak under the radar. If necessary, change the words of songs your children like to make them have better, more Biblical content.

★ **SING APPROPRIATELY:** Children continue to enjoy nursery rhymes for a long time, but if our only diet is 'childish' Christian songs, then their faith will remain at a childish level. We need to hunt out things that will be stretching, both in content, and in musical form. Often children will bring appropriate songs home from church or school, but it is worth checking out contemporary children's songs at your local Christian bookshop. Try to listen (and read the lyrics) before you buy!

★ **SING VARIETY:** Check what kind of songs your child sings at the church group they attend. Repeating these during the week has the added benefits of supporting the Sunday School teachers, and discouraging children from thinking that God is 'for Sunday only.' Try out boppy pop songs, raps, old scripture choruses, story songs and praise songs for a good balanced diet. See the list of possible resources at the end.

WHEN TO SING

You may be convinced now, but how do you get started? Here are some practical ideas to try.

★ **Sing grace:** Saying thank you before, during or after food is a good habit to get into as a family. Why not sing it occasionally. There are several you could try: Thank you for the world so sweet; Here we are together; Johnny Appleseed...

★ **Sing prayers:** For a time, my children liked to sing prayers at bedtime instead of saying them. They would just make up a tune as they talked to God. A bit hit-and-miss (and no No. 1 hits) but it gave variety to bedtime family prayers.

★ **Sing songs:** Singing songs together at bedtime can be a good additional or (occasionally!) alternative activity to reading a Bible story.

★ **Sing solos:** What about your child singing solo—performing for the others. This builds confidence and can be great fun. They may need encouragement to sing something different (or Christian). My littlest always reverts to Twinkle Twinkle Little Star, which is fine, but I am trying to wean her onto songs with more content.

★ **Sing wisely:** Action songs are great fun, but probably not for bedtime, as they are more likely to hype up than calm down.

★ **Sing in the car:** Favourite CDs for our car journeys include the soundtrack to Shrek and Remember the Lord. If you can bear the comparisons with Ned Flanders from The Simpsons, then a singalong will help to make the miles go quicker.

Resources:

CDs to try include: Remember the Lord by Colin Buchanan. The King, the snake and the promise (a Bible overview in song) and Meet the King (songs based on Mark's Gospel). All three CDs available from The Good Book Company, 0845 225 0880.

Also How Cool is That! and Praise Crazy by Johnny Burns (Integrity Media); God's Wonderful World by Julia Plaut (Kingsway Music). Available from your local Christian bookshop.

Look at www.ajoyfulnoise.net/kidspage for some interesting computer-based Karaoke Kids songs that will play on your computer!

Tim Thornborough

> By teaching and singing songs with your children, you will store up within them an easily remembered treasure house of Bible knowledge.

DAY 34 The 'god' who fell over!

Today's passages are:
Table Talk: 1 Samuel 5v1-5
XTB: 1 Samuel 5v1-5

TABLE TALK

(You need the picture or model of the ark that you made on Day 31.)

DO

The Philistines believed in a pretend god called **Dagon**. Draw and cut out a picture of Dagon's statue. As you read today's story, use your picture of Dagon, and your picture/model of the ark, to show what happened.

DAGON

READ

God is the Real King—but the Philistines don't know that yet! They think their pretend god, Dagon, helped them beat the Israelites. They're very, very wrong! **Read 1 Samuel 5v1-3**

TALK

The Philistines put the ark of God in Dagon's temple, next to their statue of Dagon. But what happened to Dagon's statue? (v3) (*It fell over!*) What did the Philistines do? (v3) (*Pick it up again!*)

READ

Read 1 Samuel 5v4-5

What happened to Dagon's statue this time? (v4) (*It fell over, and the head and hands broke off!*) Tear the head and hands off your picture of Dagon.

THINK

What did all of this show? (*That God is the Real King—not Dagon.*)

PRAY

The Philistines thought their pretend god had helped them. They were wrong! **Thank God** that nothing and no-one can stop His plans.

Building up
Read part of David's psalm of thanks in **1 Chronicles 16v23-26**. Use these words to praise **God**, the **Real King**.

DAY 35 Follow those cows!

Today's passages are:
Table Talk: 1 Samuel 6v12-16
XTB: 1 Samuel 5v6-6v16

TABLE TALK

What had the Philistines captured? (*The ark.*) They moved the ark from city to city, but wherever it went the people became **ill**. The Philistine leaders were stumped! Was it **God** making them ill??? They asked their priests what to do.

Choose two cows that have new calves.

Hitch the cows to a cart, but take their calves away.

Put the ark on the cart, and see which way the cows take it.

If they take it to Beth Shemesh, we'll know it was **God** who made us ill.

READ

Read 1 Samuel 6v12-16

Where did the cows take the ark? (v12) (*Beth Shemesh, an Israelite city.*) How did the Israelites feel when they saw the ark coming back to them? (v13) (*They rejoiced.*) The Israelites thanked God, and offered the cows as a sacrifice (gift) to Him. Who saw all this? (*See v16*)

TALK

God made those cows take the ark straight back to the Israelites! He showed the Philistines who the Real King is. Praise and thank God that He is still the Real King today.

PRAY

Building up
1 Samuel shows us that **God is the Real King**. Try to remember at least three stories that show that God is in control, and that His plans always work out. (E.g. Day 23, 29, 34)

DAYS 36-45
Notes for Parents

DAY 36
Feeling sheepish

THE BOOK OF PSALMS

Check out these descriptions of psalms. Which is right?

a) A psalm is a tree that grows in hot countries.

b) A psalm is a song or a prayer to God.

c) A psalm is a strange animal with three legs, two heads and bad breath!

Psalms are songs or prayers to God. The Israelites chanted them when they were praising God. Psalms come in different shapes and sizes. Some are long and some are short. *Find these two in the book of Psalms:*

 Psalm 117 only has _____ verses.

 Psalm 119 has _____ verses. It's very long!

Some psalms were written by someone who was _____.

Others were written when the writer was really really _____!

Over the next ten days, we're going to read several different kinds of psalms. But they have all have one thing in common.

They all praise God for being the Real King who is in control of everything!

 KEYPOINT
If you follow Jesus, you're one of God's sheep. God is like a brilliant shepherd.

Today's passages are:
Table Talk: Psalm 23v1-3
XTB: Psalm 23v1-3

TABLE TALK Read about psalms in **Notes for Parents** opposite.

READ The whole Bible tells us that **God is the Real King**. But what's it like to have God the King in charge of your life? In this psalm, David says that it's like being a <u>sheep</u> with a <u>brilliant shepherd</u> looking after you! **Read Psalm 23v1-3**

TALK Who is David's shepherd? (v1) (*The LORD*.) What do sheep need to stay alive? (*Grass, water, shelter...*) Which of these two sheep (below) is David like? (v2)

THINK God gives His people <u>everything</u> they need! He also leads them along the **right paths** (v3). What do you think that means? (*God shows His people the right way to live for Him.*)

In David's time, shepherds protected their sheep, made sure they had everything they needed, and led them the right way. God looks after His people (Christians) in the same way!

PRAY If you follow Jesus, you're one of God's sheep! Thank God for looking after you like a brilliant shepherd.

Building up
During these ten days, the Building Up task will be to read <u>all</u> of Psalm 119! Each time, jot down one thing you've learnt about God or His Word (the Bible).

Building up
See **Notes for Parents** for more about these Building Up sessions. Start by reading **Psalm 119v1-16**. Write down what you have learnt about God and/or His Word in the space on the next page.

DAYS 36-45
Notes for Parents

DAY 37
No fear!

PSALM 119

If you use the **Building Up** time to read **Psalm 119**, use this page to jot down what you learn about God and His Word.

v1–16

_____

v17–32

_____

v33–48

_____

v49–64

_____

v65–80

_____

v81–96

_____

v97–112

_____

v113–128

_____

v129–152

_____

v153–176

Today's passages are:
Table Talk: Psalm 23v4
XTB: Psalm 23v4

Talk about things that <u>frighten</u> you. (*E.g. spiders, the dark, being bullied...*) Be ready to give reassurance if needed.

In Psalm 23, David says God is like a great shepherd who looks after His sheep (Christians). But sometimes the sheep are afraid. Read v1-3 as well as v4, to remind you what a brilliant shepherd God is. **Read Psalm 23v1-4**

How does David feel? (v4) (*Unafraid and protected/comforted.*) Wow! David's not even afraid of dying! He knows that God is with him, protecting him. What comforts David and protects him? (v4) (*God's rod and staff.*)

Rods and staffs are like walking sticks! A shepherd uses them to prod sheep in the right direction and to protect them from wild animals. David knows that when he's scared, God is <u>always</u> there, guiding him and protecting him!

Who else does the Bible describe as a shepherd? Check your answer in **John 10v11**. Jesus is the Good Shepherd who died for His sheep. He died so that people like us could be with God for ever. If we trust and follow Jesus, He'll always be with us! He won't let anything happen to us that isn't part of His great plan!

Thank God that He always looks after His people.

Building up
Read Psalm 119v17-32. What have you learnt about God and/or His Word the Bible? Write your answers in the table on the left.

DAY 38
God's special guests

Today's passages are:
Table Talk: Psalm 23v5-6
XTB: Psalm 23v5-6

TABLE TALK
Talk about times when you have particularly enjoyed being someone's guest (for a meal or to stay with them). What made it special?

READ
In Psalm 23, David has been telling us how much he trusts God. And how God looks after His people like a shepherd looks after his sheep. David's enemies probably thought he was silly to trust God.
Read Psalm 23v5-6

TALK
What is God preparing for David? (v5) (*A table/banquet.*) This means a victory feast. David is God's **special guest** at this feast. God pours oil on his head to give him a special welcome. And who has to watch? (v5) (*David's enemies!*)

What follows David wherever he goes? (v6) (*God's goodness and love.*) How long will David be God's guest? (v6) (*For ever.*)

THINK
One day, all Christians will be God's guests in heaven for ever! If you are Christians, you'll be God's special guests too! It's not because we deserve it, but because **Jesus** has made it possible for us to be God's special guests.

PRAY
Thank God that He wants us to be His guests for ever in heaven.

Building up
Read Psalm 119v33-48. What have you learnt about God and/or His Word the Bible? Write your answers in the space opposite.

DAY 39
Cave cries

Today's passages are:
Table Talk: Psalm 142v1-4
XTB: Psalm 142v1-4

TABLE TALK
Who can make the saddest looking face? Now each walk round the room in a way that looks really sad.

READ
Psalm 142 is another prayer written by David to God. King Saul is jealous of David and is out to kill him. So David is hiding in a dark cave, alone and upset.
Read Psalm 142v1-4

TALK
David is very sad. What does he do? (v1-2) (*Prays to God and tells God all his problems.*) How does David feel? (v3) (*Faint and ready to give up.*) What have David's enemies done? (v3) (*Set a trap/snare for him.*) How many friends has David got to help him? (v4) (*None*)

THINK
When we're feeling down it's easy to think that God can't or won't help us. But what did David remember about God? (v3) (*God knows the way/what David should do.*) David remembered that **God is always in control**.

PRAY
What's bothering or upsetting you at the moment? Tell God all about it (as David did). Ask God to help you to keep trusting Him when you're feeling down.

Building up
Read Psalm 119v49-64. Write down anything you have learnt about God and/or His Word in **Notes for Parents** opposite.

DAY 40
Safe with God

Today's passages are:
Table Talk: Psalm 142v5-7
XTB: Psalm 142v5-7

 TABLE TALK
Talk about any caves you have visited. Were they little, large, damp, dry, safe, scary? Would they have been a good place to hide?

 READ
David is hiding from his enemies in a cave. He's very _sad_. But instead of sulking, David is asking God for help!
Read Psalm 142v5-7

 TALK
What does David say about God? (v5) (_God is his refuge/protector; and his portion/all that David needs._) What does David admit to God? (v6) (_That his enemies are too strong for him._) David admits to God that he _can't_ save himself. He **needs** God's help. What will David do when God rescues him? (v7) (_Praise God._)

 THINK
God had promised that David would one day become king. David trusted God's promise even when he was all alone and hiding in a cave. He trusted that one day he would be praising God in Jerusalem with God's people!

 PRAY
In this psalm David was very unhappy. But he knew how great it was to have God protecting him. Ask God to help _you_ to turn to Him when you're feeling sad or lonely.

Building up
Read Psalm 119v65-80. Write down anything you have learnt about God and/or His Word in **Notes for Parents** on the previous page.

DAY 41
Please forgive me

Today's passages are:
Table Talk: Psalm 130v1-4
XTB: Psalm 130v1-4

 TABLE TALK
On some paper write a list of things you need to say **sorry** to God for. Keep the list for later.

 READ
The person who wrote today's psalm is upset. He has <u>disobeyed</u> God—and he feel terrible... **Read Psalm 130v1-4**

TALK
The psalm writer cried out to God. What did he ask God to do? (v2) (_To hear his cry for mercy/help._)

What do you think **mercy** is? (_Mercy is when God does <u>not</u> give us what we deserve._) We have <u>all</u> disobeyed God and deserve to be punished. But the writer knows that we can turn to God for **forgiveness**. Even though we don't deserve it!

 THINK
In v3 what does the writer imagine God keeping? (_A record of our sins._) Imagine if God kept a **list** of <u>all</u> the times you've disobeyed Him. How long would it be? (_Mine would be huge!_) But if we say **sorry** to God and **ask** Him to forgive us, all our wrongs will be forgiven! (_More about this tomorrow..._)

Told lies
Stole sweets
Cheeky to m
Hit brother
Cheeky to a
Showed off
Disobeyed m
Grumbling
Swore
Hit brother
Cheeky to m
(aga
Lied about hom
Grumbling
Made fun of frien
Showing off
Couldn't be bothered
praying
Cheeky to mum
(again
Made fun of old
_me_
Lied to teacher
Hit brother
Kicked brothe
Moaned all da
Jealous of siste
Cheeky to teach
Selfish with swee

 PRAY
Praise God now for His amazing gift of forgiveness. <u>Say sorry</u> for the things on your list. Then <u>tear it up</u> to remind you of God's total forgiveness.

Building up
Read Psalm 119v81-96. Jot down what you have learnt about God and/or His Word in **Notes for Parents** on the previous page.

DAY 42
Watch it

Today's passages are:
Table Talk: Psalm 130v5-8
XTB: Psalm 130v5-8

 TABLE TALK

Have you ever had to stay awake all night? Why? How did you keep awake?

 READ

We're carrying on the psalm we started yesterday. The psalm writer has <u>disobeyed</u> God and he's **desperate** for God to forgive him. **Read Psalm 130v5-6**

 TALK

What does the writer say he's like? (v6) (*A watchman.*) What does a night watchman have to do? (*Stay awake all night, guarding a city or building.*) What a tiring job! How **desperate** would he be for morning to come? (*Very*)

Watchmen are <u>desperate</u> for morning to arrive, so they can finally sleep. And we should be <u>desperate</u> for God to forgive us.

 THINK

Read Psalm 130v7-8

 TALK

Who should trust God? (v7) (*Israel*) What should the Israelites trust God to do? (v8) (*Redeem/save them. 'Redeem' means to buy back.*)

God wants to save <u>us</u> too. He wants to rescue us from the punishment we deserve for sinning against Him. He wants to forgive us. God sent His Son **Jesus** to die and take the punishment we deserve.

 THINK

 PRAY

Thank God for His love that never fails (v7). Thank God that if we believe in Jesus, God will forgive us for disobeying Him.

Building up
Read Psalm 119v97-112. Write down anything you have learnt about God and/or His Word in the table on the previous page.

DAY 43
Shout it out

Today's passages are:
Table Talk: Psalm 100v1-3
XTB: Psalm 100v1-3

 TABLE TALK

Talk about things that make you <u>happy</u>, and why.

 READ

Over the last few days we've been reading <u>sad</u> psalms. But the person who wrote this one was really <u>happy</u>! **Read Psalm 100v1-3**

 TALK

What should the whole world do? (v1) (*Shout/sing for joy to God.*) What sort of songs should God's people sing to Him? (v2) (*Joyful/happy songs.*) What else does v2 say we should do? (*Worship God.*) **Worshipping God** <u>isn't</u> just singing happy songs to Him. It's living your <u>whole life</u> His way.

 READ

Read v3 again. Spot at least three great <u>reasons</u> why we should praise God. (**1**—*Because He's God. He's the Real King, in control of everything;* **2**—*God made us. We belong to Him;* **3**—*We're His people. We're His sheep.*) All Christians are God's special <u>people</u>. We're like <u>sheep</u> with a brilliant shepherd looking after us (as we saw in Psalm 23).

 PRAY

Use these three reasons to thank and praise God. Then sing a happy song for Him, too!

Building up
Read Psalm 119v113-128. Write down anything you have learnt about God and/or His Word in **Notes for Parents** on the previous page.

DAY 44
Raise the praise

KEYPOINT
God's love lasts for ever. He will never let His people down. Two more reasons to praise Him!

Today's passages are:
Table Talk: Psalm 100v4-5
XTB: Psalm 100v4-5

TABLE TALK

Play 'Guess the Building', where you give clues for the others to guess which building you're thinking about. (*E.g. school, church, supermarket, garage...*)

READ

In psalm 100, the writer is thinking about the **temple** in Jerusalem. The people would enter through outer <u>gates</u> into the temple <u>courts</u>, where they would praise God. **Read Psalm 100v4-5**

TALK

What does the psalm tell the people to do? (v4) (*Enter the temple gates with thanks and its courts with praise.*) The **temple** is where Israelites went to worship God. But we can worship God <u>anywhere</u>, not just in one special place. We don't have to wait until we're in church!

THINK

This psalm gives us more reasons to praise God. What are they? (v5) (*God is good. His love and faithfulness last for ever.*) Wow! If you're a Christian, **God will always love you!** And not just here on earth, but for ever in heaven too! And He will <u>always</u> be faithful. He'll never let His people down.

PRAY

Thank God that His love lasts for ever. Thank Him that He will never let His people down.

Building up
Read Psalm 119v129-152. Write down anything you have learnt about God and/or His Word in **Notes for Parents** next to Day 37.

DAY 45
Worldwide worship

KEYPOINT
God wants the whole world to know about Him, so that they can praise Him too.

Today's passages are:
Table Talk: Psalm 117v1-2
XTB: Psalm 117v1-2

TABLE TALK

Have a go at saying 'Praise the Lord!' in these different languages:
German: Lob den Herrn!
Dutch: Looft den Here!
French: Le Seigneur soit loué!
Spanish: El Señor sia glorificado!
Italian: Il Signore sia lodato!

READ

Psalm 117 is the <u>shortest</u> psalm. It starts and finishes with 'Praise the Lord!'. Do you know what that is in Hebrew? (*Hallelu jah!*) **Read Psalm 117v1-2**

TALK

Which parts of the world should praise God? (v1) (*All nations.*) Why should they praise God? (v2) (*Because of His love and faithfulness.*)

THINK

God wants the **whole world** to know about His love and faithfulness. He wants people everywhere to get to know Him, so that they can praise Him too. But not everyone <u>knows</u> about God's love and faithfulness, or that God is the Real King. Who needs to tell them? (*Christians— including you and me!*)

PRAY

Have <u>you</u> told anyone about God recently? If you have, pray for them now. If not, ask God to give you an opportunity to tell someone about Him this week.

Building up
Read Psalm 119v153-176. Write down what you have learnt in **Notes for Parents** next to Day 37. Now read the full list, and thank God for all that He has taught you.

DAYS 46-65
Notes for Parents

1 SAMUEL

Welcome back to the book of **1 Samuel**.

Last time, we read about **Hannah**, who was very sad because she had no children.

Hannah prayed to God, and He gave her a son—**Samuel**. Hannah had promised to give her son back to God, to serve Him, and she did. Samuel grew up in the temple, with Eli the priest.

When Samuel had grown up, he became the last Judge (leader) of the Israelites. Samuel told the Israelites God's words, and also showed them how to turn back to God when they had disobeyed Him.

Twenty years have gone by since we left the book of 1 Samuel. By now, Samuel is getting **old**. His sons are ready to lead Israel in his place—but they <u>don't</u> live for God the way that Samuel does!

Building up
Read 1 Samuel 8v6-9

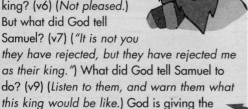

How did Samuel feel when the Israelites asked for a king? (v6) (*Not pleased.*) But what did God tell Samuel? (v7) (*"It is not you they have rejected, but they have rejected me as their king."*) What did God tell Samuel to do? (v9) (*Listen to them, and warn them what this king would be like.*) God is giving the Israelites the opportunity to turn back to Him. Tomorrow, we'll see what they decide to do...

DAY 46
A new king

KEYPOINT
The Israelites want a king to lead them. But they already have a King—God!

Today's passages are:
Table Talk: 1 Samuel 8v1-5
XTB: 1 Samuel 8v1-9

TABLE TALK

(*You need paper and pencil.*) Draw a large crown. What is this issue of Table Talk called? (*The Real King.*) Who does the Bible say is the Real King of the world? (*God*) Write **'God is the Real King'** in the middle of the crown. Put it where you'll all see it as you read 1 Samuel together.

READ

Read **Notes for Parents** to find out more about the book of 1 Samuel.

Read 1 Samuel 8v1-5

TALK

What were Samuel's sons like? (v3) (*They didn't live for God. They took bribes—money for making unfair decisions.*) The Israelites <u>didn't</u> want Samuel's sons to lead them. What <u>did</u> they want? (v5) (*A king.*)

THINK

The Israelites already had a King! <u>Who</u> was their Real King? (*God*) God has been King of the Israelites all the time. But now, they want a <u>man</u> as king instead. Does that seem silly to you? Why/why not?

God was their **perfect King**. It was so silly to turn away from Him!

God is <u>our</u> **perfect King** too! It would be silly for us to turn away from Him.

PRAY

Do you sometimes turn away from God? Do you do what <u>you</u> want, instead of what <u>God</u> your King wants you to do? If so, tell God you are sorry. Ask Him to help you to change.

Building up
See the Building Up notes in **Notes for Parents**.

DAY 47
A king's the thing

KEYPOINT
The Israelites wanted a king like the other nations, but they were supposed to be different.

Today's passages are:
Table Talk: 1 Samuel 8v19-22
XTB: 1 Samuel 8v10-22

TABLE TALK

Have you ever seen something that someone else has, and liked it so much that you want it too? (E.g. new trainers, mobile phone, puppy...) Talk about some examples.

READ

The Israelites wanted a king. So God told Samuel to tell them exactly what this king would be like. A king would make their sons and daughters work for him. He would take their best fields and vineyards. And they themselves would become his slaves. (v10-18) But the Israelites would not <u>listen</u> to the warning... **Read 1 Samuel 8v19-22**

TALK

What did the Israelites say? (v19) (*"We want a king."*) Why did they want a king so badly? (v20) (*So that they'd be like all the other nations.*)

THINK

The Israelites were **not** like other nations (people from other countries). *God* was their King. They were to obey God's rules and live for Him, so that other people would see that God is the real King. They were <u>supposed</u> to be different!

PRAY

Christians are supposed to be different too. If we obey God, and live for Him, then other people will notice. Some will ask <u>why</u> you're different. It can be hard to be different, so ask God to help you live for Him, and to be ready to tell your friends about Him when they ask <u>why</u>.

Building up
Read 1 Samuel 8v10-19. What shocking news does Samuel tell them at the end of v18? (*God will not answer their cries for help.*) Did that make them change their minds? (v19) (*No!*)

DAY 48 Disappearing donkeys

KEYPOINT
Saul searched for missing donkeys, but found Samuel instead. <u>God</u> was in control!

Today's passages are:
Table Talk: 1 Samuel 9v3-4&14-17
XTB: 1 Samuel 9v1-17

TABLE TALK

In chapter nine we meet a tall, handsome man called Saul. He doesn't know it yet, but he's going to be the first king of Israel!

READ

The story from Saul's point of view:
Read 1 Samuel 9v3-4

What had Saul's dad lost? (v3) (*Some donkeys.*) Saul searched everywhere for those missing donkeys. Did he find them? (v4) (*No*) But Saul found someone else instead... **Read 1 Samuel 9v14**

Who did Saul meet? (*Samuel*) Saul searched for <u>donkeys</u>—but found <u>Samuel</u> instead! From Saul's point of view it all looked like a **mistake**. But it wasn't...

READ

The story from God's point of view:
Read 1 Samuel 9v15-17

When did God tell Samuel about Saul? (v15) (*The day <u>before</u> Saul arrived!*) Was it an accident that Saul met Samuel? (v16) (*No, <u>God</u> sent him.*)

THINK

Wow! From Saul's point of view, his hunt for donkeys looked like a muddle. But it wasn't a muddle at all! **God** was always in control!

PRAY

God is the Real King. He is <u>always</u> in control. Thank Him for this.

Building up
Read the rest of the story in **1 Samuel 9v5-13**. Notice how God used Saul's servant (v6) and some unknown girls (v11)—as well as those disappearing donkeys!—to bring Saul to Samuel. God was totally in control!

DAY 49
Anoint him

KEYPOINT
God brought Saul to Samuel, so that Samuel could anoint Saul as king.

Today's passages are:
Table Talk: 1 Samuel 9v27–10v1
XTB: 1 Samuel 9v18–10v1

TABLE TALK

Think of some special things that are done when a new person takes over an important position (*e.g. queen, knight...*)

READ

Saul had been looking for <u>donkeys</u>—but found Samuel instead! Now he found out that Samuel was <u>expecting</u> him, and had even prepared a special meal for him! "I will explain everything in the morning", said Samuel. "And don't worry, your donkeys have been found." (v18-26) The next morning, Samuel walked with Saul to the edge of town.
Read 1 Samuel 9v27–10v1

TALK

What did Samuel say about Saul's servant? (v27) (*He was to go on ahead.*) Once the servant had gone, what did Samuel do? (v1) (*Poured oil on Saul's head, and told Saul that God was anointing him as leader.*)

THINK

To **anoint** someone means to pour <u>oil</u> on his head to show that he has been <u>chosen</u> to serve God. Being anointed was a sign to Saul that God had chosen **him** to be king.

It was **God** who brought Saul to Samuel, so that Samuel could anoint Saul as king. <u>God</u> was in control.

PRAY

God is <u>always</u> in control. How does that make you feel? Talk to God about it.

Building up
The names **Christ** (Greek) and **Messiah** (Hebrew) both mean 'the <u>anointed</u> one'. What does that tell you about Jesus? (*That He is King.*) **Jesus is God's chosen King.**

DAY 50
Wonders never cease

KEYPOINT
God gave Saul signs to help him know God had chosen him.

Today's passages are:
Table Talk: 1 Samuel 10v9
XTB: 1 Samuel 10v2-13

TABLE TALK

What do people say when something astonishing happens? (E.g. Wow!, I'm flabbergasted!, Wonders never cease...) In Bible times, they said, "Is Saul also among the prophets?" How odd! Today's story explains why...

READ

Yesterday, we read about a **sign** that God had chosen Saul to be king. What was it? (*Saul was anointed.*) Now, Samuel tells Saul some other <u>signs</u> (v2-7):

"You will meet two men, near Rachel's tomb. They will tell you that your father's donkeys have been found. Then you will meet three men. They will have three young goats, three loaves of bread and some wine. They will give you two loaves of bread. Then you will meet a group of prophets. The Spirit of the Lord will come on you, and you will prophesy with them."

Read 1 Samuel 10v9 (with older children read all of v2-9.)

TALK

How many of these signs came true? (v9) (*All of them!*) People were so <u>amazed</u> to see Saul prophesying like this (singing praise to God) that it became a catchphrase. They said, "Is Saul also among the prophets?" when they saw something amazing! (v10-13)

PRAY

God was **so kind** to Saul—giving Saul these signs to help him know that God really had chosen him. God is <u>always</u> like this. He is **so kind** to <u>us</u>, too. Think of ways God has been kind to you—then thank Him!

Building up
Table Talk Challenge: This week, when something amazing happens, say "Is Saul also among the prophets?"—and then explain why!

DAY 51
The deputy king

KEYPOINT
Saul was to be like a *deputy king*, because **God** was still the Real King.

Today's passages are:
Table Talk: 1 Samuel 10v20-25
XTB: 1 Samuel 10v14-27

TABLE TALK

Play **hangman** to guess the phrase 'The deputy king'.

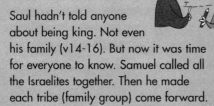

Saul hadn't told anyone about being king. Not even his family (v14-16). But now it was time for everyone to know. Samuel called all the Israelites together. Then he made each tribe (family group) come forward.
Read 1 Samuel 10v20-25

TALK

Which <u>tribe</u> was chosen? (v20) (*Tribe of Benjamin.*) Which <u>clan</u> (family) was chosen? (v21) (*Matri*) Which <u>man</u> was chosen? (v21) (*Saul*) But they couldn't find Saul! What did they do? (v22) (*They asked God.*) Where did God tell them to look? (v22) (*In the baggage/supplies.*) What did the people shout when they saw Saul? (v24) (*"Long live the king!"*)

THINK

What did Samuel explain to the people? (v25) (*Kingship/the rights and duties of a king.*) Saul was <u>not</u> to be a king like the other nations had. He was to be <u>different</u>. **God** was still the Real King. So Saul was like a *deputy king*. He had to live for God, and obey God's rules.

PRAY

Who rules your country? Pray for him or her. Ask God to help them to rule wisely, in a way that pleases God.

Building up
Read Deuteronomy 17v14-20 to find out about God's rules for <u>kings</u>. What rules can you find? As we learn more about King Saul we'll see whether he kept these rules.

DAY 52
Who will rescue JG?

KEYPOINT
Saul looked like the sort of king God wanted—He obeyed God and gave God the credit.

Today's passages are:
Table Talk: 1 Samuel 11v12-15
XTB: 1 Samuel 10v26–11v15

TABLE TALK

Read the first part of today's story in **Notes for Parents** opposite.

READ

Before the battle, some people hadn't supported Saul as king. "How can this fellow save us?", they had said. Now that Saul had won the battle, the other Israelites wanted to have these men killed... **Read 1 Samuel 11v12-15**

TALK

The other Israelites had wanted the men who hadn't supported Saul to be killed. Did Saul agree? (v13) (*No*) <u>Who</u> did Saul say had rescued Israel? (v13) (*The LORD.*) What did the people do next? (v15) (*Confirmed Saul as king, then had a great celebration!*)

THINK

Saul looked like the sort of king God wanted—one who <u>obeyed</u> God, and made sure the people knew it was **God** who rescued them. It was a <u>good start</u>. *We'll soon see if it carries on.*

PRAY

Meanwhile, ask God to help <u>you</u> to obey Him, and make sure that any glory is given to God, not you!

Building up
Read 1 Samuel 11v6 In the Old Testament, God gave His Spirit to <u>selected</u> people, who had <u>special</u> jobs. For example: **Bezalel** (Exodus 31v1-5), **Gideon** (Judges 6v34) and **Samson** (Judges 14v5-6). In 1 Samuel we see God's Spirit coming on Saul, too. But later, sadly, when Saul turns away from God, we'll see God take His Spirit away from Saul. (1 Samuel 16v14—Day 61)

DAY 52
Notes for Parents

SAUL'S STORY

Saul had been made king. Most of the Israelites were pleased. But some weren't impressed!

> How can this fellow save us? — *1 Samuel 10v27*

Now it was time for Saul's first challenge as king...

Jabesh Gilead (we'll call it **JG**) was an Israelite town, so the people living there were God's people. They were attacked by an enemy army, who trapped them inside their city.

The people of **JG** were ready to give up. But first they sent out a cry for help.

The messengers arrived at Gibeah, where Saul lived. Saul was there, ploughing the fields.

When Saul heard the news, he was furious. The Spirit of God filled Saul with power.

Saul gathered a huge army. Then he sent messengers to **JG** to tell them they were going to be saved.

Saul and his army attacked the enemy soldiers at night—and won!

You can read this part of the story in 1 Samuel 11v4-11.

DAY 53
The God who rescues

Today's passages are:
Table Talk: John 3v16
XTB: John 3v16

TABLE TALK

If you can, find a simple child's jigsaw, and time yourselves to see how quickly you can put it together.

The Bible fits together like a **Giant Jigsaw**. It shows us what God is like. We're going to jump out of 1 Samuel for a moment to see what another part of the Bible tells us about God.

READ

In yesterday's story, who did Saul say had really rescued the Israelites? (*God*) The whole Bible tells us that God is the God who *rescues*. Check out one of the most famous rescuing verses in the Bible. **Read John 3v16**

TALK

Who sent Jesus into the world? (*God*) Why did God send Jesus? (*Because He loves us.*) God loves us so much, that He sent Jesus to die for us.

DO

Use the **Book Illustration** from Day 28 to explain how Jesus died to rescue us. (If your child already knows this well, ask him/her to explain it to you instead!)

(*Optional*) Copy John 3v16 onto a large sheet of paper. Stick it where you'll all see it every day.

PRAY

Thank God that He loves you so much that He sent Jesus to rescue you.

Building up
Look up some other '3v16' verses about Jesus: **1 John 3v16**, **Luke 3v16**, and **Acts 3v16**.

DAY 54
Spot the characters

Today's passages are:
Table Talk: 1 Samuel 12v4&10-15
XTB: 1 Samuel 12v1-15

TABLE TALK
Play "Spot the Character", where you describe someone's character for the others to guess who they are. (E.g. He laughs a lot, and always forgets things; She's very kind, but keeps saying sorry.)

Now that Saul had been made king, Samuel had some important things to say to the Israelites—about characters:

ONE
Samuel's Character: First, Samuel asked the Israelites for any complaints about <u>him</u>. **Read 1 Samuel 12v4**

Had Samuel <u>cheated</u> anyone? (*No*) Had he <u>oppressed</u> them (treated them harshly)? (*No*) He'd been a good leader.

TWO
God's Character: Next, Samuel reminded the Israelites of God's character. God was **good** to His people. But they <u>kept</u> turning away from Him. They prayed to pretend gods (like Baal) instead. So God allowed their enemies to defeat them. **Read 1 Samuel 12v10-11**

What did the people do? (v10) (*Cried out to God.*) How did God answer? (v11) (*By sending rescuers, like Gideon.*)

THREE
The People's Character: Lastly, Samuel reminded the people of what <u>they</u> were like. **Read 1 Samuel 12v12-15**

Now the people had a <u>choice</u>: Serve and obey God, and all will be well (v14). <u>Or</u> Turn against God, and He'll turn against them (v15). Ask God to help <u>you</u> choose the first option (to serve and obey Him).

PRAY

Building up
How would you describe <u>your</u> character? Thank God for the good parts of your character, and ask Him to help you change any parts that need changing.

DAY 55
Thunder bolt

Today's passages are:
Table Talk: 1 Samuel 12v16-19&22
XTB: 1 Samuel 12v16-25

TABLE TALK
(You need pencil and paper.) List some things you've learnt about God from 1 Samuel. (*E.g. God is the Real King, God is the God who rescues, God's words always come true…*)

READ
The Israelites still needed to learn more about God's character…
Read 1 Samuel 12v16-19

TALK
What time of year was it? (v17) (*Dry season, when the wheat was harvested.*) But what did God send? (v18) (*Thunder and rain.*) The people were scared! What did they ask Samuel? (v19) (*To pray for them.*) What had they realised at last? (v19) (*How wrong they were to demand a king.*)

READ
Samuel told the people not to be afraid. Then he told them something wonderful about God's character. **Read 1 Samuel 12v22**

What would God <u>not</u> do? (v22) (*He would not reject/abandon His people.*)

DO
Write **'God will never abandon His people'** on your list.

PRAY
Look at your list again. These things were all true at the time of 1 Samuel. But **God doesn't change!** So these things are as true <u>now</u> as well. Thank God for these truths about Him.

Building up
Read 1 Samuel 12v20-25 What did Samuel say he would do for the people? (v23) (*Pray for them and teach them.*) What did he tell the people to do? (v24) (*Serve God faithfully and remember the great things God had done for them.*) How can <u>you</u> obey v24? Ask God to help you.

DAY 56
Saul slips up

KEYPOINT
Saul disobeyed God, so God took away the right of Saul's family to be kings of Israel.

Today's passages are:
Table Talk: 1 Samuel 13v5-14
XTB: 1 Samuel 13v1-15

TABLE TALK
On Day 51, we called Saul 'the deputy king". Why? (*Because <u>God</u> is the Real King. Saul had to obey God's rules.*)

Samuel had given Saul a very clear rule to obey: **Read 1 Samuel 10v8**

How long was Saul to wait? (*7 days.*)

READ
Saul and his son Jonathan got an army together and attacked the Philistines. But the Philistines had an army too...
Read 1 Samuel 13v5-7

TALK
How big was the Philistine army? (v5) (*HUGE!*) How did the Israelites feel? (v7) (*Terrified*)

READ
Before a battle, God's people would offer <u>sacrifices</u> (gifts) to show they trusted God. But only the <u>priest</u> (Samuel) was allowed to do it. Saul <u>waited</u> for Samuel as he'd been told. The 7th day came—but Samuel didn't...
Read 1 Samuel 13v8-14

TALK
Who made the offerings? (v9) (*Saul*) Who arrived just afterwards? (v10) (*Samuel*) The 'deputy king' <u>disobeyed</u> the Real King. So what did God do? (v13-14) (*God took away the right of Saul's family to be kings of Israel.*) Someone else would be king instead. We'll meet him soon...

Think of some ways you have disobeyed God this week. (*E.g. telling lies, not being kind, gossiping...*) Say sorry to God. Ask Him to help you change.

PRAY

Building up
We're going to jump to chapter 15 tomorrow. If you have time, read part of what will be missed, about Saul's son Jonathan, in **1 Samuel 14v1-23**.

DAY 57
What's that bleating?

KEYPOINT
Saul disobeyed God again. The way to please God is to listen to His word and obey it.

Today's passages are:
Table Talk: 1 Samuel 15v13-15&22
XTB: 1 Samuel 15v1-23

TABLE TALK
Take it in turns to mimic the sound of an animal for the others to guess. Include some unusual ones like grasshoppers! We're skipping ahead a few chapters to see how Saul <u>disobeys</u> God again. This time, Saul is caught out by sheep bleating and cows mooing!

READ
God had a task for Saul to do. He was to attack and completely destroy the city of Amalek. Saul attacked Amalek, as he was told, and destroyed <u>most</u> things—but he <u>kept</u> the best sheep and cattle.
Read 1 Samuel 15v13-15

TALK
What did Samuel ask Saul? (*See v14.*) What reason did Saul give for keeping the sheep and cattle? (v15) (*To offer as a sacrifice to God.*)

Saul's answer 'sounds' good—but Samuel wasn't impressed! **Read v22**. What did Samuel say was <u>better</u> than sacrifices? (*<u>Obeying</u> God*)

THINK
Saul should have **listened** to God's words and **obeyed** them. But he didn't! Saul <u>rejected</u> God's commands—so God <u>rejected</u> Saul as king (v23).

PRAY
What really pleases God? It's when we obey what we read in the Bible, and live our lives for Him. Ask God to help you to please Him this week.

Building up
Does destroying a whole city sound too harsh? **Read v1-2** to see why God said it. (*Because of the way the Amalekites had attacked God's people in the past.*) This was God's <u>judgment</u> on them, just as He had said would happen. (See Exodus 17v8-16 and Deuteronomy 25v17-19 for God's original commands.)

DAY 58
That's torn it

KEYPOINT
God tore the kingdom away from Saul. Someone else would be king, who <u>would</u> obey God.

Today's passages are:
Table Talk: 1 Samuel 15v27-29&35
XTB: 1 Samuel 15v24-35

Recap: What did Saul do wrong in yesterday's story? (*Kept sheep and cattle he should have destroyed.*)

Saul had <u>disobeyed</u> God's commands. So Samuel told Saul that God had rejected him as king. As Samuel turned to leave, Saul grabbed hold of Samuel's robe...
Read 1 Samuel 15v27-29

What happened to Samuel's robe? (v27) (*It tore.*) What did Samuel say? (v28) (*That God had torn the kingdom of Israel away from Saul, and given it to someone better than him.*) Then Samuel said something important about God. What was it? (v29) (*God doesn't lie or change His mind.*) Wow! That means we can always trust God to do what He says!

There's sad ending to this story.
Read v35

How did **Samuel** feel about Saul? (*He mourned/grieved for him.*) How did **God** feel about Saul? (*He was sorry that He had made Saul king.*)

This story shows us that God is <u>upset</u> when people turn away from Him. It also tells us that God <u>never lies</u>, or changes His mind. How do these two things make you feel? Talk to God about them.

Building up
Read v28 again. The new king would be 'better' than Saul. Think of some ways in which he could be better. (*E.g. obeyed God, cared about God being praised rather than himself, helped his people to love and obey God...*)

DAY 59
King of hearts

KEYPOINT
'Man looks at the outward appearance, but God looks at the heart.' 1 Samuel 16v7

Today's passages are:
Table Talk: 1 Samuel 16v1-3&6-7
XTB: 1 Samuel 16v1-7

Look at the parcels in **Notes for Parents**. What do you think each one holds? Crack the codes to find out.

You can't always tell what's on the <u>inside</u> by looking at the <u>outside</u>! Samuel needed to learn that too...
Read 1 Samuel 16v1-3

Whose son had God chosen to be the new king? (v1) (*One of <u>Jesse's</u> sons.*) What did God tell Samuel to take with him? (*Oil*) Samuel was to use the oil to <u>anoint</u> one of Jesse's sons as the new king.

Samuel told everyone that he'd come to offer a sacrifice (gift) to God. He invited Jesse and his sons. When they arrived, Samuel was very impressed with Jesse's oldest son, **Eliab**. He was tall and handsome... **Read 1 Samuel 16v6-7**

Had God chosen Eliab? (v7) (*No*) Why not? (v7) (*Because God looks inside.*)

God doesn't worry about the <u>outside</u> (how tall or good looking we are). God looks at what we're like <u>inside</u> (whether we love God and trust and obey Him.) How does that make you feel?

What do you want <u>your</u> heart to be like? Talk about it together, and write your answers in the heart opposite.

Ask God to help you to be like this.

Building up
'Man looks at the outward appearance, but God looks at the heart.' 1 Samuel 16v7
Copy this onto a large sheet of paper. Learn it together as a memory verse. Test each other on it during the day.

DAYS 59-60
Notes for Parents

DAY 60
A heart for God

KEYPOINT
God chose Jesse's youngest son, David, to be the new king.

CRACK THE CODE
Have a guess at what each parcel holds. Then crack the code to see if you were right.

B D E G I L M O P R S T U W
↗ ↘ ⇩ ⇦ ⬆ ↘ ⬇ ⬅ ↖ ▽ ▷ ◁ ▽ ◁

Today's passages are:
Table Talk: 1 Samuel 16v8-13
XTB: 1 Samuel 16v8-13

DO

(*You need pencil and paper.*) Draw a row of <u>seven</u> stick men. Jesse and his seven sons were invited by Samuel to a sacrifice. God had told Samuel that one of Jesse's sons would be the new king.

READ

Yesterday, 𝕏𝕏𝕏𝕏𝕏𝕏𝕏 we saw that God had <u>not</u> chosen Eliab, the eldest son. *Cross out one stick man.*
Read 1 Samuel 16v8-10

TALK

Did God choose Abinadab? (v8) (*No*) *Cross out a stick man.* Did God choose Shammah? (v9) (*No*) *Cross out a stick man.* Did God choose any of the next four sons? (v10) (*No*) *Cross out four more stick men.*

READ

They had run out of sons!!!
Read 1 Samuel 16v11-13

TALK

The <u>youngest</u> son hadn't been invited. Where was he? (v11) (*Taking care of the sheep.*) What was his name? (v13) (*David*) What did God say about David? (v12) (*"Anoint him. He's the one!"*) So Samuel anointed David with oil, to show that God had chosen David to be the next king.

THINK

David was the <u>youngest</u> son. He hadn't even been invited to the sacrifice. But what does **God** look at? (*The heart.*) As we'll see soon, David's heart <u>loved</u> and <u>trusted</u> God.

PRAY

Look again at the heart you filled in yesterday. Is this how your hearts have been since then? If so, thank God. If not, ask Him to help you change.

Building up (Day 60)
Look how this part of Old T history is summed up in the New T in **Acts 13v20-23**. How is David described? (v22) (*'A man after God's own heart.'*) A much greater King was one of David's descendants. Who was He? (v23) (*Jesus*)

Building up
See Building Up notes opposite.

DAY 61
Harp of the matter

KEYPOINT
God provided a way for David to live in the palace—even though it seemed impossible.

Today's passages are:
Table Talk: 1 Samuel 16v14-23
XTB: 1 Samuel 16v14-23

TABLE TALK

What instruments can you play? (*Piano? Drums? Recorder? Kazoo?*) Do you know what instrument <u>David</u> played? (*The harp.*)

READ

God had chosen **David** to be the next king. The Spirit of God was with David. But how could an ordinary, unknown shepherd boy become king? It seems **impossible!** Today, we see the first small step in David becoming king...
Read 1 Samuel 16v14-17

TALK

Saul was in a mess. He had turned away from God, so God had punished him by taking away His Holy Spirit from Saul. Now Saul was being bothered by an evil spirit instead. What did Saul need? (v15) (*Someone who can play the harp.*) Who do you think that would be? (*David!*)

Read 1 Samuel 16v18-23

Did Saul like David? (v21) (*Yes*) Whenever the evil spirit bothered Saul, David played his harp. How did Saul feel then? (*Better*)

THINK

Wow! Saul had invited David into his palace! God's plans for David to become king were starting to work out. The impossible was beginning to happen!

SING

Sing a song about how <u>great</u> God is. Thank Him that His plans always work out. Even when it seems impossible!

Building up
David wrote nearly half of the songs in the book of Psalms (73 of them). Read one of the most famous—**Psalm 23**. Maybe you could sing it together!

DAY 62
Battle stations

READ

The Israelites were at war with the Philistines. The Israelite army was on one hill, with the Philistine army on another. There was a valley between them.

The Philistines had a HUG[E] champion called Goliath.

READ

Read 1 Samuel 17v4-7 (with older children read the whole story in v1-24)

TALK

How tall was Goliath? (v4.) (*Over nine feet/nearly three metres.*) Goliath looked terrifying in his bronze armour! BUT do you remember what **1 Samuel 16v7** says? (*'Man looks at the outward appearance, but God looks at the heart.'*) The <u>outward</u> appearance—like how tall and scary someone looks!—**doesn't matter!** It's what's <u>inside</u> that counts.

Building up
Do you remember David's oldest brother, **Eliab**? Look again at what God said about him in **1 Samuel 16v7**, then read **1 Samuel 17v1[3]**

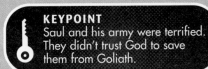

KEYPOINT
Saul and his army were terrified. They didn't trust God to save them from Goliath.

Today's passages are:
Table Talk: 1 Samuel 17v4-7&20-24
XTB: 1 Samuel 17v1-24

DAY 63
Spot the difference

KEYPOINT
David trusted that the LORD would give him victory over Goliath.

Today's passages are:
Table Talk: 1 Samuel 17v26&32-37
XTB: 1 Samuel 17v25-37

TABLE TALK

Saul and his army were all terrified of Goliath!

Goliath challenged the Israelites to fight him. But they were all too scared!

Think of some differences between David and Goliath. (*E.g. Goliath is bigger, older and a Philistine.*)

READ

The most important difference was <u>inside</u> them... **Read 1 Samuel 17v26**

READ

David's oldest brothers were in Saul's army. So Jesse (David's dad) sent David to see them, and take them some food.
Read 1 Samuel 17v20-24

TALK

Heathen (or uncircumcised) meant that Goliath didn't believe in God. What did David say Goliath was doing? (v26) (*Defying the army of the living God.*) When Goliath defied (challenged) <u>God's army</u>, he was really defying <u>God</u>! The HUGE difference between David and Goliath was that **David** loved and trusted God. But **Goliath** didn't.

What did the Israelites do when they saw Goliath? (v24) (*Ran away in terror!*)

THINK

Saul and his army were <u>terrified</u>. They didn't <u>trust</u> God to save them from Goliath. They'd forgotten that **God is the Real King**. No Philistine (no matter how tall!) was a match for God!!!

READ

King Saul heard what David had said, and sent for him.
Read 1 Samuel 17v32-37

What had David killed? (v36) (*Lions and bears.*) But that's <u>not</u> why David was so confident! Who did David trust to give him victory? (v37) (*The LORD.*)

PRAY

Is there anything you are worried or scared about? Ask God to help you to remember that **He** is the Real King. Ask Him to help you to <u>trust</u> Him.

PRAY

Ask God to help <u>you</u> to love and trust Him like David did.

...ab was in Saul's army. But (like the rest of Saul's ...ay), he <u>wouldn't</u> fight Goliath. That shows that ...b would have been a bad choice as king. In his ...rt, Eliab didn't trust God to help him beat Goliath.

Building up
There's more evidence that Eliab would not have been a good choice as king. **Read 1 Samuel 17v26-30** to see what Eliab's heart was like.

DAY 64
Giant killer

KEYPOINT
Goliath had defied God. So God gave David an amazing victory.

Today's passages are:
Table Talk : 1 Samuel 17v38-51
XTB : 1 Samuel 17v38-51

DO

Act out today's story as you read it. If you have one child, they can be David. If you have two, they can act both David and Goliath. Any others can be Saul (v38) or Philistines (v51).

Read 1 Samuel 17v38-40

What did Saul want David to have? (v38) (*His armour.*) But David said No. What did David take with him? (v40) (*His staff, sling and five stones.*)

It looked like it would be a Knock-Out for Goliath. But Goliath had defied **God**. BIG MISTAKE!!!

READ

Read 1 Samuel 17v41-51

TALK

Goliath fought with a spear, javelin and sword. But how was David fighting? (v45) (*In the name of Almighty God.*) David slung one stone at Goliath. Where did it hit? (v49) (*Goliath's forehead.*)

THINK

Look at the pics at the top of yesterday's page. It <u>looked</u> like a Knock-Out. BUT Goliath had challenged **God**! And David was fighting for God's honour. So God gave David an amazing victory.

PRAY

God is <u>far</u> greater than any human— even a giant like Goliath! Nobody and nothing can challenge God! He's the greatest! Thank and praise Him now.

Building up
David knew that God is far greater than any human. Read one of David's songs of praise to God in **Psalm 8**.

DAY 65
The whole world

KEYPOINT
The whole world knows the story of David & Goliath. It shows that God is the Real King.

Today's passages are:
Table Talk : 1 Samuel 17v46
XTB : 1 Samuel 17v46

TABLE TALK

Did you know the story of David and Goliath <u>before</u> reading it in Table Talk? It one of the best known stories in the Bible **Read 1 Samuel 17v46** to see why.

TALK

Who did David want to know about God (v46) (*The whole world.*)

What other Old T stories do you know? See if your child can finish all these titles:
• **Noah**'s _____ (*Ark/boat*)
• **Joseph** and his _____ (*many coloured or long sleeved coat*)
• **Moses** crossing the _____ (*Red Sea*)
• **Jonah** and the _____ (*whale/big fish*)
• **Daniel** in the _____ (*lion's den*)

THINK

All of these Old Testament stories show us that **God is the Real King**. That's something that the <u>whole world</u> needs to know!

PRAY

What country do <u>you</u> live in? Name at least five people who help you to learn about God, the Real King. Pray for those people now. Thank God for them and as Him to help them.

Building up
Who do you know who tells people in anothe country about God? Pray for them now. Plan a way to contact them this week (e.g. letter, email, phone call...) to tell them what you have been learning in Table Talk. Remember to tell them that you've been <u>praying</u> for them, too.

Extra Readings

WHY ARE THERE EXTRA READINGS?

Table Talk and **XTB** both come out every three months. The main Bible reading pages contain material for 65 days. That's enough to use them Monday to Friday for three months.

Many families find that their routine is different at weekends from during the week. Some find that regular Bible reading fits in well on school days, but not at weekends. Others encourage their children to read the Bible for themselves during the week, then explore the Bible together as a family at weekends, when there's more time to do the activities together.

The important thing is to help your children get into the habit of reading the Bible for themselves—and that they see that regular

Bible reading is important for **you** as well.

If you **are** able to read the Bible with your children every day, that's great! The extra readings on the next page will augment the main **Table Talk** pages so that you have enough material to cover the full three months.

You could:

• Read **Table Talk** every day for 65 days, then use the extra readings for the rest of the third month.

• Read **Table Talk** on weekdays. Use the extra readings at weekends.

• Use any other combination that works for your family.

DAVID'S SONGS

On Days 36 to 45 we dipped into the book of Psalms. In these 26 extra readings, we're going to look at five more psalms. All five were written by King David.

There are 26 Bible readings on the next three pages. Part of each verse has been printed for you—but with a word missing. Fill in the missing words as you read the verses. Then see if you can find them all in the wordsearch.

Note: Some are written backwards—or diagonally!!

K	D	E	S	E	R	V	E	G	M	I	G	H	T	Y
H	I	G	H	A	T	L	O	R	U	N	L	O	R	D
V	A	N	D	A	V	I	D	E	L	M	O	S	E	S
F	O	R	G	I	V	E	S	A	L	L	R	X	T	B
T	H	I	C	K	X	S	T	T	C	E	Y	E	H	A
T	H	R	O	N	E	S	H	N	A	G	O	K	O	N
C	N	E	W	O	N	E	I	E	L	O	V	E	U	S
E	H	A	Y	W	E	T	N	S	L	O	W	Y	G	W
F	M	U	M	W	O	R	D	S	A	D	L	Y	H	E
R	D	A	D	E	K	A	W	A	X	T	B	X	T	R
E	O	K	D	A	R	K	N	E	S	S	U	N	S	E
P	R	O	M	I	S	E	S	C	R	E	A	T	E	D

Extra Readings

Psalm 145

1 ☐ **Read Psalm 145v1-3**

Every day, David wanted to praise (exalt) God the real King—because God is so great. Will you?
"Great is the LORD and most worthy of praise; His **g** _ _ _ _ _ _ _ _ _ _ is beyond understanding." (v3)

2 ☐ **Read Psalm 145v4-7**

Adults will tell children about God's wonderful deeds (one generation telling the next—v4). Thank God for the people who tell you about Him.
"What you have done will be praised from one generation to the next; they will tell of your **m** _ _ _ _ _ acts." (v4)

3 ☐ **Read Psalm 145v8-12**

God is compassionate/merciful. This means He helps us, and doesn't treat us the way we deserve.
"The LORD is gracious and compassionate, **s** _ _ _ _ to become angry and rich in love." (v8)

4 ☐ **Read Psalm 145v13**

God is the real King. His kingdom lasts for ever.
"Your rule is eternal, and you are **K** _ _ _ for ever." (v13)

5 ☐ **Read Psalm 145v13-16**

God always keeps His promises.
"The LORD is faithful to all His **p** _ _ _ _ _ _ _ _ and loving towards all He has made." (v13)

6 ☐ **Read Psalm 145v17-21**

David knew that God always hears our prayers, and gives us loving answers.
"The LORD is near to all who **C** _ _ _ on Him." (v18)

Psalm 19

7 ☐ **Read Psalm 19v1-6**

The sky shows us what God is like—how great and powerful He is.
"How clearly the sky reveals God's **g** _ _ _ _ !" (v1)

8 ☐ **Read Psalm 19v7-11**

This part of David's song is all about God's word to us (your Bible may use words like law, teachings, statutes, commands etc). God's word is pure, perfect, true, trustworthy and right.
"The law of the LORD is **p** _ _ _ _ _ _ ." (v7)

9 ☐ **Read Psalm 19v12-14**

David knows that he says and thinks wrong things. He asks God to help him to please God with what he does, says and thinks (v14). Pray this for yourself, too.
"May my **W** _ _ _ _ and thoughts be pleasing in your sight, O LORD." (v14)

Psalm 103

10 ☐ **Read Psalm 103v1-5**

David knows that God will provide all his needs—and that God is the only One who can forgive his sins.
"He **f** _ _ _ _ _ _ _ all my sins." (v3)

Extra Readings

11 ☐ **Read Psalm 103v6-7**

When the Israelites were slaves in Egypt, God chose Moses to lead them. God rescued them with amazing miracles.

"He made known His ways to

M _ _ _ _ , His deeds to the people of Israel." (v7)

12 ☐ **Read Psalm 103v8-10**

David knows that God shows HUGE kindness to His people, when they don't deserve it. (The Bible calls this _grace_.) Thank God for being like this.

"He does not treat us as our sins

d _ _ _ _ _ _ _ ." (v10)

13 ☐ **Read Psalm 103v11-14**

God's love is higher and greater than we can ever imagine!

"As **h _ _ _** as the sky is above the earth, so great is His love for those who honour Him." (v11)

14 ☐ **Read Psalm 103v15-18**

People only live for a fairly short time (like flowers that grow for a while and then die). But God's love lasts for EVER!

"But for those who honour the LORD, His

l _ _ _ lasts for ever." (v17)

15 ☐ **Read Psalm 103v19-22**

God is the real King. Everything in heaven and on earth should praise Him.

"The LORD has placed His **t _ _ _ _ _** in heaven; He is king over all." (v19)

Psalm 34

16 ☐ **Read Psalm 34v1-3**

David wanted to praise God at _all times_. When could you praise God today? At breakfast? In school? Walking home? On your bike? In bed? Try and do all of them!

"I will praise the LORD at

a _ _ times." (v1)

17 ☐ **Read Psalm 34v4-7**

When David prayed, God answered him. We sometimes forget how _amazing_ prayer is. God is the real King, and Creator of the Universe. Yet He _listens_ when we talk to Him, and _answers_ our prayers. Thank Him!

"I prayed to the LORD and He

a _ _ _ _ _ _ _ me." (v4)

18 ☐ **Read Psalm 34v8-10**

God is _good_. And He gives _good_ answers to our prayers.

"Taste and see that the LORD is

g _ _ _ ." (v8)

19 ☐ **Read Psalm 34v11-14**

If we want to honour God (v11), we should live in a way that pleases Him. Ask God to help you to do this.

"Keep your tongue from evil and your lips from speaking **l _ _ _** ." (v13)

20 ☐ **Read Psalm 34v15-22**

Are you sad, worried or scared? Whatever the problem, you can _always_ turn to God for help. He is close to the broken-hearted (v18).

"The **L _ _ _** is close to the broken-hearted and saves those who are crushed in spirit." (v18)

Extra Readings

Psalm 139

21 ☐ Read Psalm 139v1-6

God knows <u>everything</u> about you. He knows what you are doing right now. And He knows the next words you will say!

"Even before I speak, You already **k** _ _ _ what I will say." (v4)

22 ☐ Read Psalm 139v7-12

God is <u>everywhere</u>. He is with you wherever you go. He can even see you in the pitch dark!

"Even **d** _ _ _ _ _ _ _ is not dark for You." (v12)

23 ☐ Read Psalm 139v13-16

God knew all about you before you were even born!

"You **c** _ _ _ _ _ _ _ every part of me; you put me together in my mother's womb." (v13)

24 ☐ Read Psalm 139v17-18

God isn't like us. He is all powerful, all knowing, totally wonderful. And this amazing God is always with us!

"When I **a** _ _ _ _ , I am still with You." (v18)

25 ☐ Read Psalm 139v19-22

These verses seem hard. But David knows that people who hate God will be punished. Unless they turn away from their sins, and turn to God for forgiveness, then their punishment will be death.

"They say wicked things about You; they speak evil things against your **n** _ _ _ ." (v20)

26 ☐ Read Psalm 139v23-24

God wants the very best for you. Ask Him to show you how you should change, to live your life in a way that pleases Him.

"Search me. O God, and know my heart; test me, and discover my **t** _ _ _ _ _ _ _ ." (v23)

WHAT NEXT?

We hope that **Table Talk** has helped you get into a regular habit of reading the Bible with your children.

Table Talk comes out every three months. Each issue contains 65 full **Table Talk** outlines, plus 26 days of extra readings. By the time you've used them all, the next issue will be available.

Available from your local Christian bookshop—or call us on **0845 225 0880** to order a copy.

COMING SOON!
Issue Nine of Table Talk

Issue Nine of Table Talk explores the books of John and 2 Samuel, and dips into some of Paul's letters as well.

- The Gospel of **John** tells us all about Jesus. Read about some of the miracles that pointed to <u>who</u> Jesus is.
- Find out more about King David in the book of **2 Samuel**.
- Read one of Paul's prison letters.